THE MONEY-SAVING GARDEN YEAR

Laura O. Henderson

Table of Content

INTRODUCTION

The Mindset of a Money-Saving Gardener....................................6

The joy of growing more while spending less...................................6
How frugality and sustainability go hand in hand............................9
Essential tools & techniques for a cost-conscious gardener...........13
A quick-start seasonal overview of the book...................................18

CHAPTER 1

January: Planning for a Frugal Year..22

Setting a garden budget & savings goals..22
Choosing cost-effective crops 27
Making a seed inventory & organizing leftovers............................36
Sourcing free and cheap seeds 39
DIY seed-starting mix & homemade seed trays.............................41

CHAPTER 2

February: Seed Starting & Smart Purchases................................45

When to buy vs. when to DIY 45
Best frugal sources for soil, compost, and amendments...............51
Creating a garden layout to maximize space & resources.............54
Winter sowing: The ultra-cheap cold stratification method..........57
Planning succession planting for continuous harvests..................60

CHAPTER 3

March: Maximizing Free Resources..65

The best free soil amendments..65
The power of composting: Making "black gold" for free................70
Mulching on a budget...72

Finding free or low-cost plants..73
DIY greenhouse ideas from salvaged materials..........................74

CHAPTER 4
April: Smart Planting & Waste Reduction..................................77

Direct sowing vs. transplanting: Saving money with the right approach...77
How to grow your own mulch and fertilizer................................79
Free water sources & rainwater collection systems...................80
Repurposing household waste into garden tools & plant supports..82
Extending the life of seedlings..82

CHAPTER 5
May: Growing Food for Free (or Almost Free)............................84

Perennial edibles: Invest once, harvest for years........................84
The easiest plants to grow from kitchen scraps.........................86
Companion planting for pest control..89
The no-cost way to create a self-seeding garden.......................92
Upcycled trellises & vertical gardening solutions......................95

CHAPTER 6
June: The Peak Harvest—Saving & Preserving..........................100

Freezing, drying, and fermenting: Budget-friendly food preservation..100
Building a DIY solar dehydrator...104
Making your own organic fertilizers from garden waste............109
The cheapest way to stake, cage, and support plants...............114
Free pest control strategies..118

CHAPTER 7

July: Keeping the Garden Thriving Without Extra Costs....................123

Water-saving techniques The best homemade plant foods...................123
How to avoid costly summer garden mistakes 126
Pruning for productivity 128
Making the most of second-season planting 132

CHAPTER 8

August: Seed Saving & Perennial Propagation..138

Saving seeds from common vegetables and herbs...................................138
Dividing perennials for more free plants...140
Propagating fruit trees and berry bushes from cuttings.........................142
How to store seeds for maximum viability..145
Budget-friendly ways to prepare for the fall garden................................147

CHAPTER 9

September: Free Fertilizers & Fall Prep..150

DIY organic compost teas for soil health..150
Collecting and using leaf mold (nature's free mulch)...............................153
Best free and cheap cover crops for soil improvement...........................155
Smart end-of-season seed swaps...156
Preparing a no-cost compost pile for winter...157

CHAPTER 10

October: ECONOMICAL Garden Clean-Up & Soil Building................160

Using fall leaves to enrich garden beds...160
Low-cost ways to protect plants from frost...162

Making cold frames from salvaged windows..163
DIY row covers for season extension..165
Storing root crops without expensive equipment.....................................166

CHAPTER 11
November: Extending the Harvest & Prepping for Winter..................167

Cheap & easy ways to insulate raised beds..167
How to build a low-cost winter greens garden..169
Making homemade potting soil for next year...170
Reusing and cleaning old seed trays & containers....................................172
What to buy now for next year at deep discounts....................................173

CHAPTER 12
December: Reflection & Smart Planning for Next Year........................175

Reviewing what worked & what didn't...175
Budget-friendly garden gifts & holiday projects.......................................177
Best winter reading for frugal gardeners..178
Planning next season's no-cost experiments...180
Where to get free or discounted seeds & plants for next year...............181

BONUS SECTIONS

50+ DIY Gardening Hacks That Save Money..184
The Best Free & Cheap Gardening Resources..188
Garden Expense Tracker & Budgeting Worksheets...................................192
A Year of Garden Projects Using Salvaged & Free Materials..................200

INTRODUCTION

THE MINDSET OF A MONEY-SAVING GARDENER

A great garden doesn't have to cost a fortune. In fact, with the right mindset, it can be one of the most rewarding and cost-effective ways to provide fresh food, enhance your landscape, and support a sustainable lifestyle. A money-saving gardener sees value in every seed, repurposes materials creatively, and maximizes nature's free resources—water, compost, and biodiversity—to grow abundance without waste.

This book will guide you through a year of frugal gardening, showing you how to cut costs without cutting corners. You'll learn how to grow high-yield crops, source free or cheap materials, and turn everyday waste into valuable garden assets. Whether you're starting with a small backyard plot or an expansive food garden, adopting a resourceful, DIY approach will help you grow more while spending less. Each month, we'll explore budget-friendly gardening strategies tailored to the season. By the end of the year, you'll have built not just a thriving garden, but a sustainable, cost-effective gardening habit that saves money year after year.

THE JOY OF GROWING MORE WHILE SPENDING LESS

There is a deep and abiding joy in stepping into a garden teeming with life—lush tomato vines climbing toward the sun, lettuce beds brimming with crisp greens, and fruit trees heavy with the season's bounty. But that joy is multiplied tenfold when you realize that this abundance was cultivated not with costly inputs or expensive tools, but through knowledge, resourcefulness, and a little creative ingenuity.

I learned this lesson the hard way. When I first started gardening, I was swept up in the illusion that success required a hefty investment. I bought premium compost, name-brand fertilizers, and every shiny new gadget promising bigger yields. My first season, while productive, left me with a painful realization—my grocery bill had shrunk, but my gardening expenses had skyrocketed. Wasn't this supposed to save me money?

Determined to do better, I committed to a different approach the next year: growing more while spending less. Instead of store-bought amendments, I built a compost system, turning kitchen scraps and yard waste into nutrient-rich soil. I swapped seeds with fellow gardeners rather than purchasing new ones. I learned the art of propagating cuttings and dividing perennials, transforming a handful of plants into an entire landscape. That year, my harvest was just as abundant—perhaps even more so—but my expenses had plummeted.

The Power of Small, Smart Choices

A money-saving garden isn't built overnight, nor does it rely on deprivation. Instead, it thrives on smart, intentional choices that compound over time. When you learn to make the most of free resources, nature rewards you with exponential growth.

- **A Single Seed Becomes a Hundred** – Saving seeds from one plant can yield an entire season's worth of produce the following year. I still remember the first time I let my cilantro bolt and set seed, expecting little. Months later, after a gentle rain, I was stunned to find dozens of volunteer seedlings pushing through the soil—an effortless second harvest, free of charge.

- **Soil Health Without the Price Tag** – Healthy soil is the foundation of a thriving garden, but it doesn't require expensive amendments.

I once spent a summer collecting fallen leaves, layering them into my garden beds along with grass clippings and kitchen scraps. By spring, those materials had broken down into rich, dark humus—feeding my plants better than any store-bought fertilizer ever had.

- **Multiplication Through Propagation** – Some of the best plants in my garden weren't purchased; they were shared. A single cutting of rosemary from a neighbor became an entire hedge, just as a gifted clump of chives multiplied into a thick border around my vegetable beds. Learning to propagate plants was like unlocking a secret code to infinite abundance.

Simplicity Over Excess

Many new gardeners fall into the trap of overcomplication—believing that success requires the latest tools, specialty soil blends, or expensive raised beds. But the most productive gardens are often the simplest. Some of the highest-yielding plots I've ever seen were tended by those who relied on traditional, time-tested methods rather than modern conveniences.

Take, for instance, my experience with trellising. Early on, I spent a small fortune on metal cages for tomatoes, only to watch them buckle under the weight of the vines. Frustrated, I turned to a cheaper (and surprisingly more effective) alternative—staking branches pruned from a neighbor's tree and weaving them into a sturdy support system. The result? A functional, rustic trellis that not only saved me money but blended beautifully into the garden.

The Freedom of a Self-Sustaining Garden

Perhaps the greatest joy of growing more while spending less is the independence it cultivates. A frugal garden isn't dependent on the whims of the market, nor is it vulnerable to supply chain disruptions or inflation. It is a living, breathing ecosystem that provides year after year, powered by natural cycles and careful stewardship.

I remember the first time I realized my garden had reached a state of self-sufficiency. My compost was nourishing the soil, my saved seeds were sprouting new generations of crops, and my self-seeding flowers and herbs were returning without any intervention. I had built something that would continue to provide—without the constant need for spending.

This is the essence of gardening wisely. It's not about deprivation, but about working in harmony with nature rather than against it. It's about seeing value where others see waste, about turning the ordinary into the extraordinary. And most importantly, it's about growing a garden that enriches both the soil and the soul—without emptying your wallet.

Because in the end, the true reward of gardening isn't just in the harvest. It's in the knowledge that you've cultivated abundance through patience, wisdom, and a deep respect for the natural world.

HOW FRUGALITY AND SUSTAINABILITY GO HAND IN HAND

Frugality in the garden isn't just about cutting costs—it's about working smarter, using what nature freely provides, and creating a system that sustains itself over time. At its core, a frugal garden is a sustainable garden. Every dollar saved is often a resource conserved, a waste stream reduced, or a natural cycle restored.

I didn't always see the connection between frugality and sustainability. Early in my gardening journey, I assumed that going "green" meant investing in expensive organic products, fancy compost tumblers, and costly rainwater collection systems. But as I sought to lower my gardening expenses, I stumbled upon a truth that changed everything: the most sustainable solutions are often the cheapest ones.

The less I relied on store-bought inputs, the more I worked with nature's rhythms—and the healthier my garden became. The more I reused and repurposed, the more I realized how wasteful traditional gardening practices could be. By making budget-conscious choices, I was also making eco-friendly ones.

Compost: The Ultimate Example of Frugality and Sustainability

Composting is a perfect example of how saving money aligns with sustainability. Instead of spending on expensive bags of fertilizer or hauling away kitchen scraps, a frugal gardener turns waste into gold.

I remember my first attempt at composting—an unsightly pile of kitchen scraps and leaves tucked in a forgotten corner of my yard. I worried it wouldn't work without one of those pricey tumblers or commercial compost starters. But nature proved me wrong. With nothing more than time, microbes, and occasional turning, the pile broke down into rich, dark soil that transformed my garden beds. I had created a self-sustaining nutrient cycle—without spending a cent.

This is the essence of a frugal-sustainable garden: using what you have, rather than buying what you don't need.

Water Conservation: Saving Money While Protecting a Precious Resource

Water is essential for any garden, but it doesn't have to come from a hose attached to a high utility bill. Many traditional watering methods are both expensive and wasteful—sprinklers that drench sidewalks, evaporation-prone overhead watering, and reliance on municipal water during droughts.

When I sought to reduce my water costs, I unknowingly stepped into more sustainable practices. Rainwater collection became a simple way to store free, unchlorinated water. Mulching with leaves and grass clippings helped retain soil moisture, reducing the need for irrigation. Deep watering techniques encouraged roots to grow stronger, making plants more resilient.

Every method that saved me money also made my garden more drought-resistant and self-sustaining. I no longer had to depend on a constant supply of tap water because my garden had learned to hold onto moisture naturally.

Seed Saving: A Timeless Tradition of Frugality and Resilience

Seed saving is both a lost art and a revolutionary act. Before industrial agriculture, gardeners and farmers relied on the seeds they had—carefully selecting the strongest plants, allowing them to go to seed, and saving them for the next season.

When I first began gardening, I spent a small fortune on seed packets each year. But then I noticed something remarkable—nature was offering me free seeds at every turn. Tomatoes dropped overripe fruit, and seedlings sprouted where I hadn't planted them. Basil and dill scattered their seeds, creating new patches of herbs without any effort on my part.

Once I embraced seed saving, my gardening costs plummeted, and my plants became more resilient. My homegrown seeds adapted to my soil and climate, outperforming store-bought varieties. I no longer relied on commercial seed companies, and I was contributing to biodiversity rather than depleting it. What began as a way to save money turned into a way to preserve plant heritage and strengthen my garden's natural cycles.

Repurposing & Upcycling: Turning Waste into Garden Gold

A frugal gardener sees value where others see waste. Raised beds don't have to be built from expensive lumber—they can be made from salvaged bricks, logs, or even old dresser drawers. Plant labels don't need to come in a plastic-wrapped package; they can be cut from yogurt containers or wooden spoons.

One of my proudest garden projects was a trellis built entirely from discarded materials. I found an old wooden ladder by the roadside, removed the broken rungs, and wove together some twine I had saved from hay bales. The result was a sturdy pea and bean trellis that cost me nothing—and kept waste out of the landfill.

Sustainable gardening is about more than just reducing waste; it's about rethinking how we interact with materials. Instead of feeding the cycle of consumption, a frugal gardener finds creative ways to use what already exists.

The Long-Term Rewards of a Frugal, Sustainable Garden

The true beauty of a money-saving, self-sustaining garden is that it only gets better over time. The longer you cultivate soil health, the richer and more fertile it becomes—eliminating the need for synthetic fertilizers. The more you practice seed saving, the more your crops adapt and thrive. The more you mulch, compost, and recycle natural resources, the less reliant you become on outside inputs.

One of my greatest joys as a gardener is seeing how my space has transformed over the years. What once required heavy inputs and constant tending now flourishes with minimal intervention. My soil is alive with microbes, my plants are strong, and my expenses are almost nonexistent.

This is the magic of frugality and sustainability working together. It's not about sacrificing quality—it's about building a garden that lasts, where nature and nurture work in harmony. It's about stepping out of the cycle of endless spending and into a world where abundance comes not from a shopping cart, but from the earth itself. Because in the end, the most rewarding harvest isn't just the food on your plate—it's the knowledge that you've built something truly self-sufficient, resilient, and in tune with the rhythms of nature.

ESSENTIAL TOOLS & TECHNIQUES FOR A COST-CONSCIOUS GARDENER

A cost-conscious gardener doesn't need an arsenal of expensive tools or a shed overflowing with gadgets. In fact, some of the most effective gardening methods require nothing more than a sharp eye for repurposing, a bit of ingenuity, and a willingness to work with nature rather than against it.

Early in my gardening journey, I fell into the trap of believing that success required high-end tools. I purchased ergonomic trowels, collapsible raised beds, self-watering planters, and specialty pruning shears—only to realize later that many of these tools were unnecessary. As I shifted toward a more frugal and sustainable approach, I discovered that the best tools were often the simplest and that a handful of smart techniques could replace expensive inputs entirely.

Below are the essential tools and techniques every budget-conscious gardener should embrace—items that offer long-term value, methods that maximize efficiency, and approaches that help you save money while growing an abundant garden.

Essential Gardening Tools: Buy Once, Use For A Lifetime
A gardener only needs a few well-chosen tools to accomplish nearly every task in the garden. Instead of buying every new gadget on the market, invest in high-quality basics that last for decades.

1. The Sturdy Hand Trowel – The Workhorse of the Garden

A good hand trowel is essential for planting, digging, and transplanting. Look for one with a solid, rust-resistant blade and a comfortable grip. Avoid flimsy, decorative options that bend under pressure. My favorite trowel? A secondhand stainless-steel one I found at a garage sale for a fraction of the price of a new one—still going strong after ten years.

2. A Quality Pair of Pruners – Precision Over Power

Sharp, well-made pruning shears are indispensable for trimming, harvesting, and shaping plants. Bypass pruners (which cut like scissors) are best for live growth, while anvil pruners work well for dry branches. A well-maintained pair can last a lifetime if cleaned and sharpened regularly. I've used the same pair for over a decade, occasionally disassembling it for a quick sharpening rather than replacing it.

3. The Multi-Purpose Hori Hori Knife – The Ultimate Garden Tool

If I had to choose just one tool for the garden, it would be my hori hori knife. This Japanese digging knife is a powerhouse—acting as a trowel, weeder, pruner, and measuring tool all in one. It's an investment, but one that replaces several tools, making it an ideal choice for a budget-conscious gardener.

4. A Strong Garden Fork – The Secret to Healthy Soil

Instead of buying a rototiller (which is expensive, noisy, and disrupts soil structure), invest in a sturdy digging fork. It aerates soil, loosens compacted beds, and helps mix in compost—all without disturbing beneficial soil microbes. I bought mine secondhand from a retiring gardener, and it remains one of my most-used tools.

5. The Humble Bucket – A Gardener's Best Friend

A simple 5-gallon bucket is one of the most versatile (and cheapest) tools in any garden. It can be used for carrying compost, mixing soil, collecting weeds, and even as a makeshift watering can. Many businesses give away buckets for free—bakeries, delis, and restaurants often discard food-grade ones that can be repurposed.

6. A Durable Watering Can or Hose with a Shut-Off Valve

Watering efficiently saves money and resources. A high-quality watering can (often found at thrift stores) ensures gentle watering, while a hose with a shut-off valve prevents unnecessary water waste. Rainwater collection further reduces reliance on municipal water, cutting costs even more.

Cost-Saving Techniques That Reduce Tool Dependence

Rather than relying on expensive solutions, a cost-conscious gardener prioritizes techniques that make gardening easier, more productive, and less reliant on commercial products.

1. No-Till Gardening – Let Nature Do the Work

Tilling the soil every season requires heavy equipment and can lead to long-term soil degradation. Instead, embrace no-till gardening:

- Layer compost, mulch, and organic matter on top of the soil rather than digging it in.
- Allow earthworms and microbes to naturally improve soil structure.
- Reduce labor and avoid the need for expensive fertilizers.

Since adopting no-till methods, I've seen my soil become richer each year—without the cost of renting a tiller or buying synthetic amendments.

2. Mulching for Moisture Retention and Weed Suppression

Mulching is one of the most effective ways to reduce both labor and expenses in the garden. A thick layer of organic material (straw, leaves, wood chips, or grass clippings) locks in moisture, suppresses weeds, and enriches the soil as it breaks down. Instead of buying commercial mulch, I use free materials:

- Leaves collected in fall (neighbors are often happy to give them away).
- Grass clippings from my own lawn.
- Wood chips from local tree services, which often deliver them for free.

This simple practice eliminates the need for store-bought mulch and reduces my watering needs dramatically.

3. Companion Planting for Natural Pest Control

Instead of purchasing chemical pesticides or expensive organic sprays, use nature's built-in pest management system—companion planting. Some plants naturally repel pests, attract beneficial insects, or improve the health of their neighbors. A few examples:

- **Marigolds** deter aphids and nematodes.
- **Basil** enhances tomato growth and repels mosquitoes.
- **Nasturtiums** act as a trap crop for aphids.
- **Garlic and onions** repel common garden pests like carrot flies and cabbage moths.

Since implementing companion planting, I've saved money on pest control while increasing my yields—a win-win for both my garden and my budget.

4. DIY Fertilizers and Soil Amendments

Instead of purchasing costly fertilizers, use simple, homemade alternatives:

- **Banana peel tea** (soak banana peels in water) for potassium.
- **Eggshell powder** (crushed eggshells) for calcium.
- **Compost tea** (steeping finished compost in water) for an all-purpose plant boost.
- **Diluted coffee grounds** to improve soil acidity and add nitrogen.

These methods provide all the nutrients my plants need, without a single dollar spent on commercial fertilizers.

5. Propagation: Turn One Plant Into Many

Why buy new plants each season when you can multiply what you already have? Learning to propagate plants through cuttings, division, and layering has saved me hundreds of dollars over the years.

- **Softwood cuttings** from herbs like rosemary and mint root easily in water.
- **Dividing perennials** (hostas, daylilies, chives) creates multiple plants from one.
- **Layering** (bending a stem to the soil to encourage rooting) works well for blackberries and raspberries.

A single gifted strawberry plant turned into an entire bed within a few seasons—just by letting runners take root naturally.

Smart Gardening for Lifelong Savings

A cost-conscious gardener isn't one who sacrifices quality, but one who prioritizes efficiency, sustainability, and creativity. By investing in a few high-quality tools and embracing simple, effective techniques, you can cultivate a thriving, productive garden without unnecessary expenses.

Over the years, my approach has evolved from spending freely to gardening with intention—learning that the most valuable tools aren't always the most expensive ones and that nature itself provides many of the solutions we seek. A frugal gardener isn't just saving money; they're creating a system that grows stronger, richer, and more self-sustaining with each passing season. And that, more than any store-bought tool, is the greatest investment of all.

A QUICK-START SEASONAL OVERVIEW

A thriving, budget-friendly garden follows nature's rhythms. Each season presents unique opportunities to save money, maximize yields, and prepare for future success. This quick-start overview outlines key frugal gardening tasks for each season, ensuring that every effort builds upon the last for year-round abundance.

Spring: Laying the Foundation Without Overspending

Spring is a season of renewal, planning, and preparation. Rather than rushing to the garden center, a cost-conscious gardener focuses on using free or low-cost methods to build soil health, start seeds, and establish a strong foundation.

Key Tasks:

- **Soil Preparation:** Use homemade compost, leaf mold, and natural amendments instead of expensive fertilizers.
- **Seed Starting:** Begin seeds indoors under natural light or near a sunny window to avoid costly nursery transplants.
- **Tool Maintenance:** Clean and sharpen existing tools instead of replacing them.
- **Weed Prevention:** Apply free mulch (leaves, straw, grass clippings) to suppress weeds before they take over.
- **Rainwater Collection:** Set up free or low-cost rain barrels to reduce water bills in the coming months.
- **Early Crops:** Direct sow hardy vegetables like peas, spinach, and radishes to maximize harvests.

Summer: Maximizing Yields While Minimizing Costs

With plants in full growth, summer is a time for maintenance, harvesting, and strategic planning. A frugal gardener focuses on efficiency—reducing water usage, controlling pests naturally, and preserving excess harvests for future seasons.

Key Tasks:

- **Water Wisely:** Use drip irrigation, deep watering techniques, and mulch to retain moisture and cut down on water costs.
- **Weed Control:** Continue mulching and hand-pulling weeds to avoid reliance on costly herbicides.
- **Pest Management:** Implement companion planting, introduce beneficial insects, and use DIY organic sprays instead of commercial pesticides.
- **Harvest and Preserve:** Pick fruits and vegetables at peak ripeness and preserve the surplus through freezing, drying, or fermenting.
- **Succession Planting:** Replant quick-growing crops like lettuce, beans, and carrots for an extended harvest.
- **Seed Saving:** Begin collecting seeds from healthy plants to avoid buying new ones next season.

Fall: Extending the Growing Season and Preparing for the Next Year

As temperatures cool, fall is a critical time for preparing the garden for winter while continuing to harvest and plant cold-hardy crops. A well-managed fall garden reduces costs in the following seasons.

Key Tasks:

- **Extend the Season:** Use row covers, cold frames, or DIY hoop houses to continue growing greens and root crops.
- **Plant Perennials:** Establish fruit trees, berry bushes, and perennial herbs while the soil is still warm.
- **Compost and Mulch:** Build compost piles with fall leaves and spread mulch over garden beds to enrich the soil.
- **Garlic and Cover Crops:** Plant garlic and nitrogen-fixing cover crops (like clover or rye) to improve soil fertility over winter.
- **Tool Storage:** Clean, oil, and store tools properly to extend their lifespan.

Winter: Planning, Learning, and Budgeting for the Year Ahead

Though the garden may be dormant, winter is the ideal time to plan for next season, build new skills, and source free or discounted materials.

Key Tasks:

- **Review and Plan:** Reflect on successes and challenges from the past year and create a budget-conscious plan for the next season.
- **Order Seeds Strategically:** Take inventory of saved seeds and order only what's necessary, focusing on heirloom and high-yield varieties.
- **Build and Repair:** Use downtime to construct raised beds, trellises, or compost bins from reclaimed materials.
- **Learn and Network:** Read books, join local gardening groups, and exchange seeds or cuttings with fellow gardeners.
- **Start Indoor Herbs or Microgreens:** Grow nutrient-dense greens indoors to continue harvesting fresh food year-round.

Year-Round Gardening with a Frugal Mindset

Each season presents opportunities to grow more while spending less. By planning ahead, using natural resources, and applying simple yet effective techniques, a money-saving gardener builds a self-sustaining system that becomes more abundant with each passing year. Whether just starting out or refining an existing garden, this seasonal approach ensures a productive, low-cost garden that thrives in every season.

CHAPTER 1

JANUARY: PLANNING FOR A FRUGAL YEAR

January is the gardener's quiet season—a time to dream, plan, and set the foundation for a productive, budget-conscious year. While the garden rests, a frugal gardener focuses on strategic planning, seed inventory, and sourcing free or low-cost materials. Thoughtful preparation now prevents unnecessary expenses later and ensures that every dollar spent in the coming months contributes to long-term success.

This month is all about setting clear goals, maximizing resources, and finding creative ways to grow more while spending less. By prioritizing efficiency and sustainability, January's planning efforts will lead to a thriving, cost-effective garden all year long.

SETTING A GARDEN BUDGET & SAVINGS GOALS

A well-planned garden is a productive garden, and that planning begins long before the first seed is planted. Just as a gardener maps out plant spacing and seasonal rotations, financial planning is equally crucial for long-term success. A thoughtfully crafted garden budget ensures that every dollar is spent wisely, while strategic savings goals help create a self-sustaining, resource-efficient space that flourishes year after year.

Many gardeners, myself included, start out with excitement and enthusiasm, only to realize later that impulse purchases and hidden costs can add up quickly. I remember my first full growing season—what started as a modest backyard vegetable patch quickly spiraled into unexpected expenses. I eagerly bought every organic soil amendment, specialty seed variety, and "must-have" tool, convinced they were necessary for success. By midsummer, my budget was stretched thin, and I found myself questioning whether I had gained more than I had spent.

That season taught me a valuable lesson: gardening doesn't have to be expensive to be productive. The most abundant gardens aren't built on endless spending but on thoughtful resource allocation, creative problem-solving, and a mindset of working with nature rather than against it. Through trial and error, I learned to set clear financial boundaries, source free and low-cost materials, and focus my spending on investments that would yield long-term rewards.

Below, we'll explore the key components of an effective garden budget, strategies to save money while maximizing yields, and practical steps to set savings goals that support a self-sustaining garden.

1. Understanding Your Garden's Financial Needs

Before setting a budget, it's essential to understand where money is typically spent in a garden. By breaking down costs into categories, you can identify areas where expenses can be reduced or eliminated.

Common Gardening Expenses:

1. **Seeds & Plants** – Seed packets, starter plants, fruit trees, perennials
2. **Soil & Amendments** – Compost, mulch, fertilizers, soil testing kits
3. **Tools & Equipment** – Hand tools, watering cans, hoses, trellises, raised beds
4. **Irrigation & Water Costs** – Rain barrels, drip irrigation systems, municipal water usage
5. **Pest & Weed Control** – Organic sprays, row covers, mulch

6. **Garden Structures** – Greenhouses, cold frames, fences, garden beds
7. **Preservation Supplies** – Canning jars, dehydrators, fermenting kits

Once you have a clear understanding of these categories, you can prioritize spending on essentials while reducing or eliminating unnecessary costs.

2. Setting a Realistic Garden Budget

A garden budget should be both realistic and flexible, accounting for seasonal needs while allowing room for unexpected opportunities. The best approach is to create a simple budget that aligns with your overall financial goals.

Steps to Create a Garden Budget:

1. **Assess Past Spending (If Applicable)** – Review previous gardening expenses to identify patterns and areas for improvement.
2. **Set a Total Budget Limit** – Determine a comfortable spending range for the year (e.g., $100, $500, $1,000).
3. **Prioritize Essential Expenses** – Allocate funds to must-haves (e.g., seeds, soil amendments, water conservation tools).
4. **Identify Cost-Cutting Opportunities** – Explore DIY alternatives, secondhand tools, and free resources.
5. **Track Spending Throughout the Season** – Keep a simple record of purchases to stay within budget.

Example Budget Breakdown (for a $250 yearly budget):

- Seeds & Plants: **$50** (focus on seed-saving and plant swaps)
- Soil Amendments: **$40** (homemade compost, minimal store-bought inputs)

- Tools: **$30** (thrifted or secondhand)
- Water Conservation: **$50** (DIY rain barrel, soaker hoses)
- Pest & Weed Control: **$30** (companion planting, DIY sprays)
- Miscellaneous: **$50** (unexpected needs)

This structured approach ensures that every dollar is spent intentionally, allowing the garden to thrive without financial strain.

3. Strategies to Reduce Gardening Costs Without Sacrificing Quality

A frugal gardener maximizes resources, embraces self-sufficiency, and looks for creative ways to reduce spending while maintaining high productivity.

Cost-Saving Strategies:

- **Start Seeds Instead of Buying Plants** – A single seed packet costs the same as one nursery plant but produces dozens of seedlings.
- **Save and Exchange Seeds** – Develop a habit of collecting and storing seeds to eliminate yearly seed costs.
- **Make Your Own Compost** – Kitchen scraps, leaves, and grass clippings create nutrient-rich soil without purchasing commercial fertilizers.
- **Use Free or Upcycled Materials** – Repurpose household items for plant containers, trellises, and garden edging.
- **Invest in Perennials** – Fruit trees, berry bushes, and perennial herbs offer a return year after year.
- **Water Efficiently** – Collect rainwater, use drip irrigation, and mulch heavily to minimize water costs.
- **Practice Companion Planting** – Natural pest deterrents reduce the need for expensive sprays and interventions.

By integrating these strategies, a gardener can drastically cut costs while improving the garden's long-term sustainability.

4. Setting Savings Goals for Long-Term Investments

While frugality is essential, there are times when a well-planned investment leads to greater savings over time. Setting specific savings goals allows gardeners to invest in high-impact, long-lasting improvements.

Examples of Smart Garden Investments:

- **Rainwater Collection System** – A $100 investment can replace years of municipal water costs.
- **Cold Frames or Greenhouses** – Extending the growing season saves money on grocery store produce.
- **High-Quality Tools** – Durable tools reduce replacement costs over time.
- **Fruit Trees & Perennials** – A $30 tree produces fruit for decades, providing long-term savings.

How to Set a Garden Savings Goal:

1. **Identify the Investment** – Choose a one-time purchase that offers long-term value.
2. **Determine the Cost** – Research the best price and alternatives (DIY, secondhand, free options).
3. **Create a Savings Plan** – Set aside small amounts each month (e.g., saving $10/month for a $120 rain barrel system).
4. **Track Progress & Adjust as Needed** – If an unexpected expense arises, shift priorities but stay committed to long-term savings.

By planning for these investments in advance, gardeners can improve efficiency and productivity without financial stress.

The Power of Financially Intentional Gardening

Setting a garden budget and savings goals transforms gardening from a costly hobby into a financially sustainable lifestyle. By focusing on necessity over impulse, using creative cost-saving techniques, and investing strategically, a gardener can cultivate abundance without financial burden.

The shift from reactive spending to intentional budgeting has completely changed the way I approach gardening. I no longer feel pressured to buy every new product or tool; instead, I focus on building a resilient, self-sufficient system where every dollar and every resource is used wisely.

The most rewarding gardens aren't those built on extravagant spending, but those cultivated with foresight, resourcefulness, and a deep respect for the natural abundance that gardening provides. With a thoughtful financial plan, a garden can yield not just food, but financial freedom, sustainability, and a lifetime of harvests.

CHOOSING COST-EFFECTIVE CROPS: HIGH-YIELD, LOW-MAINTENANCE, MULTI-PURPOSE

A frugal garden is not just about cutting costs—it's about maximizing returns. The best way to do this is by selecting crops that produce abundantly, require minimal input, and serve multiple functions. Whether you have a small backyard, a sprawling food forest, or a few containers on a balcony, the right plant choices can provide food, improve soil, and reduce future expenses.

The most cost-effective crops share three key traits:

1. **High-Yield** – Producing a large harvest per plant or per square foot.
2. **Low-Maintenance** – Requiring little watering, fertilization, or pest control.
3. **Multi-Purpose** – Serving multiple roles, such as food, soil enrichment, or companion planting.

1. High-Yield Crops: Grow More in Less Space

Crops that produce a high yield ensure you get the most food per plant or per square foot. These are the best choices for gardeners who want to save money on groceries while making efficient use of their space.

Top High-Yield Crops & Best Growing Techniques

1. Leafy Greens (Lettuce, Spinach, Kale, Swiss Chard)

- **Why They're Cost-Effective:** Fast-growing, continuous harvest, nutrient-dense.
- **Best Techniques:**
    - **Cut-and-Come-Again Harvesting:** Instead of pulling the whole plant, pick outer leaves regularly to extend the harvest for months.
    - **Succession Planting:** Sow new seeds every 2-3 weeks to ensure a continuous supply.
    - **Shade in Summer:** Use partial shade to prevent bolting in hot weather.

Lettuce

2. Tomatoes (Indeterminate Varieties Like 'Cherry' or 'San Marzano')

- **Why They're Cost-Effective:** One plant can produce 10–20 pounds of fruit.
- **Best Techniques:**
    - **Vertical Growing:** Use trellises or cages to maximize space and improve airflow.
    - **Prune Suckers:** Removing side shoots focuses energy on fruit production.
    - **Deep Planting:** Bury stems deeply to encourage strong root growth.

Tomato

3. Zucchini & Summer Squash

- **Why They're Cost-Effective:** A single plant can produce dozens of fruits over the season.
- **Best Techniques:**
    - **Hand Pollination:** If fruit isn't forming, manually transfer pollen between male and female flowers.
    - **Succession Planting:** Start new plants mid-season to replace aging ones.
    - **Mulch Heavily:** Helps retain moisture and prevents powdery mildew.

Zucchini

4. Beanws (Bush & Pole Varieties)

- **Why They're Cost-Effective:** High yields, nitrogen-fixing (improves soil fertility).
- **Best Techniques:**
    - **Companion Planting:** Grow with corn and squash (Three Sisters Method) for natural support and pest control.
    - **Frequent Harvesting:** Pick young pods regularly to encourage continuous production.
    - **Trellising Pole Beans:** Increases yield per square foot and improves air circulation.

5. Potatoes & Sweet Potatoes

- **Why They're Cost-Effective:** High-calorie staple, stores well, easy to propagate from scraps.

- **Best Techniques:**
    - **Grow in Containers or Towers:** Saves space and increases yields.
    - **Use Straw Mulch:** Reduces weeding and protects tubers from sunlight.
    - **Hilling Up Soil:** Encourages more tuber formation.

2. Low-Maintenance Crops: Maximum Output, Minimal Effort

Low-maintenance crops require little care once established, making them ideal for frugal gardeners who want reliable harvests without constant upkeep.

Top Low-Maintenance Crops & Best Growing Techniques

1. Perennial Herbs (Rosemary, Thyme, Oregano, Chives, Mint)

- **Why They're Cost-Effective:** Live for years, need little water, repel pests, and provide culinary and medicinal benefits.
- **Best Techniques:**
    - **Mulch Heavily:** Retains moisture and reduces weeding.
    - **Prune Lightly:** Regular harvesting encourages bushier growth.
    - **Divide & Replant:** Many herbs, like chives and mint, spread easily and can be divided to create more plants.

2. Garlic & Onions

- **Why They're Cost-Effective:** Low-maintenance, stores well, repels pests.
- **Best Techniques:**
    - **Plant in Fall for Bigger Bulbs:** Overwintering leads to larger harvests.

- **Mulch to Suppress Weeds:** Reduces the need for weeding and conserves moisture.
- **Use for Pest Control:** Interplant with vegetables like carrots and tomatoes to repel pests naturally.

3. Berries (Strawberries, Raspberries, Blackberries)

- **Why They're Cost-Effective:** Perennials that produce fruit for years with minimal care.
- **Best Techniques:**
  - **Mulch with Straw or Pine Needles:** Keeps berries clean and prevents weeds.
  - **Prune Annually:** Increases fruit production and prevents disease.
  - **Propagate for Free Plants:** Runners (strawberries) and canes (raspberries) can be divided to expand the patch at no cost.

4. Rhubarb & Asparagus (Perennial Vegetables)

- **Why They're Cost-Effective:** Planted once, harvested for decades.
- **Best Techniques:**
  - **Wait Before Harvesting:** Allow plants to establish for 1–2 years before picking.
  - **Divide Every Few Years:** Keeps plants productive and allows for propagation.
  - **Heavy Mulching:** Reduces weeds and retains moisture.

Rhubarb

3. Multi-Purpose Crops: Maximize Function & Value

Some plants offer multiple benefits beyond just food production. These crops provide soil enrichment, natural pest control, or medicinal uses—saving money in multiple ways.

Top Multi-Purpose Crops & Best Growing Techniques

1. Legumes (Peas, Beans, Clover)

- **Why They're Cost-Effective:** Fix nitrogen in the soil, improving fertility for future crops.
- **Best Techniques:**
    - **Use as Cover Crops:** Grow in fall/winter to replenish soil nutrients.

- **Chop & Drop Method:** Cut plants back and leave roots in place to decompose.

2. Sunflowers

- **Why They're Cost-Effective:** Provide edible seeds, attract pollinators, and act as natural trellises for climbing plants.
- **Best Techniques:**
  - **Use for Living Trellises:** Grow beans or cucumbers alongside.
  - **Harvest Seeds for Food & Future Planting:** A single sunflower can yield hundreds of seeds.

3. Pumpkins & Winter Squash

- **Why They're Cost-Effective:** Store for months, provide edible seeds, and their large leaves suppress weeds.
- **Best Techniques:**
  - **Grow on Compost Piles:** Takes advantage of excess nutrients.
  - **Use as a Ground Cover:** Reduces evaporation and blocks weeds.

Strategic Plant Choices for Maximum Savings

By selecting high-yield, low-maintenance, and multi-purpose crops, a gardener can create an abundant, self-sustaining garden that requires minimal financial input. Pairing these crops with the right techniques—such as succession planting, vertical gardening, and companion planting—ensures maximum productivity without unnecessary expenses.

A cost-effective garden isn't about growing everything—it's about growing the right things, in the right way, for the highest return. With careful planning and smart crop selection, any gardener can enjoy a season of plentiful harvests while keeping costs to a minimum.

MAKING A SEED INVENTORY & ORGANIZING LEFTOVERS

A well-organized seed inventory is the foundation of a cost-effective garden. It prevents unnecessary purchases, ensures you use seeds before they expire, and allows for better planning throughout the year. A neglected box of half-used seed packets can quickly lead to waste, disorganization, and forgotten varieties. With a structured approach, you can keep your seeds viable, accessible, and ready for planting when the time comes.

Why a Seed Inventory Matters

Many gardeners, even experienced ones, fall into the trap of overbuying seeds or forgetting what they already have. A good inventory system helps you:

- **Avoid unnecessary spending** – Knowing what you have prevents duplicate purchases.
- **Plan effectively** – You can easily see what's available for upcoming seasons.
- **Keep seeds viable** – Proper storage extends the life of seeds, ensuring strong germination rates.
- **Share and swap** – Having an organized system makes it easier to trade extras with fellow gardeners.

Step 1: Gathering & Assessing Your Seeds

The first step is to gather all your seeds in one place. This includes packets from previous years, leftover seeds from planting, and any newly purchased or swapped varieties.

Once collected, assess their condition:

- **Check expiration dates** – Most seeds remain viable for 1-5 years, depending on the type.
- **Inspect for damage** – Look for mold, moisture exposure, or insect damage.
- **Conduct a germination test** – If unsure of viability, place a few seeds on a damp paper towel and check for sprouting in a few days.

Step 2: Categorizing for Easy Access

Organizing seeds by category makes it easier to find what you need quickly. Consider sorting them in ways that make sense for your gardening style:

- **By Plant Type:** Vegetables, herbs, flowers, perennials, and cover crops.
- **By Planting Season:** Cool-season crops (lettuce, kale, carrots) vs. warm-season crops (tomatoes, peppers, beans).
- **By Expiry Date:** Prioritize using older seeds first.

Step 3: Choosing a Storage System

Good seed storage extends viability and prevents exposure to moisture, pests, and temperature fluctuations. Here are a few effective storage solutions:

- **Airtight containers** – Mason jars, plastic bins, or metal tins protect from humidity.
- **Zip-lock bags with silica packets** – These absorb excess moisture and prevent mold.
- **Accordion file organizers** – Label sections for different seed types or planting months.

- **Old photo albums or baseball card holders** – Perfect for keeping seed packets visible and tidy.

Regardless of the method, store seeds in a **cool, dry, and dark** place—such as a basement, pantry, or refrigerator.

Step 4: Creating a Seed Inventory Log

Keeping a written or digital record of your seeds ensures you always know what's available. An effective seed log should include:

- **Seed name & variety** – "Brandywine Tomato" vs. "Roma Tomato."
- **Purchase or harvest date** – Helps track seed age and viability.
- **Germination rate** – Results from testing, if applicable.
- **Expected expiry** – Reference a seed viability chart for longevity.
- **Notes** – Special requirements, successes, or failures from previous plantings.

A simple notebook works, but digital spreadsheets (Google Sheets, Excel) allow for easy sorting and long-term tracking.

Step 5: Managing Leftover Seeds

After organizing, you'll likely have partially used packets. Instead of discarding them:

- **Repack and reseal** – If packets are damaged, transfer seeds to labeled envelopes.
- **Share and swap** – Join local gardening groups or online seed exchanges.
- **Freeze long-term storage seeds** – Place in a vacuum-sealed bag in the freezer for extended viability.
- **Plan around them** – Prioritize using older seeds in your next planting cycle.

SOURCING FREE AND CHEAP SEEDS & DIY SEED-STARTING MIX WITH HOMEMADE SEED TRAYS

Sourcing Free and Cheap Seeds

Seeds are the foundation of every garden, but they don't have to be a major expense. With the right strategies, you can acquire seeds for free or at a very low cost, allowing you to expand your garden without breaking the budget. By tapping into community resources, seed swaps, and even harvesting your own, you can build a diverse seed collection that keeps giving year after year.

1. Save Seeds from Your Own Garden

One of the simplest ways to get free seeds is by saving them from plants you already grow. Many vegetables, herbs, and flowers produce seeds that can be collected, stored, and replanted in future seasons.

- **Easy-to-save vegetable seeds** – Tomatoes, peppers, beans, peas, lettuce, and squash are beginner-friendly.
- **Self-seeding flowers and herbs** – Calendula, marigolds, dill, basil, and cilantro readily drop seeds for the next season.
- **Biennials & perennials** – Carrots, onions, and kale require two years to produce seeds but are worth the effort.

To ensure strong, healthy plants, save seeds only from the most vigorous specimens in your garden. Dry them completely before storing in labeled envelopes or airtight jars.

2. Join Seed Swaps & Community Exchanges

Seed swaps are one of the best ways to acquire a variety of seeds at no cost. These can be local events, online forums, or organized swaps within gardening groups.

- **Local gardening clubs** – Many community gardens and horticulture societies host seed swaps.
- **Online platforms** – Websites like Seed Savers Exchange, Permies.com, and Facebook gardening groups often have members willing to trade seeds.
- **Library seed banks** – Many public libraries now offer seed libraries where you can "borrow" seeds, grow them, and return seeds from your harvest.

When participating in a swap, ensure that seeds are properly labeled and include information about growing conditions, variety, and harvest year.

3. Find Discounted & Clearance Seeds

Timing your seed purchases strategically can save significant money. Many garden centers and online retailers offer deep discounts at certain times of the year.

- **End-of-season sales** – Late summer and fall are the best times to find clearance seeds.
- **Bulk seed purchases** – Some companies sell seeds in bulk at lower prices, ideal for staple crops.
- **Last season's seed stock** – Even though many seeds have expiration dates, they often remain viable for years. Stores will discount older packets even when they are still good.

4. Get Free Seeds from Nonprofit Organizations

Several organizations distribute free seeds to encourage gardening, sustainability, and food security. Some of the best sources include:

- **The Free Seed Project** – Provides free seeds to those interested in growing food.

- **Native plant initiatives** – Some conservation groups give away native seeds to promote pollinator-friendly gardens.
- **Extension services & universities** – Agricultural programs often provide free sample seeds for testing new varieties.

Checking with local botanical gardens, extension offices, or food security programs can reveal additional free seed opportunities in your area.

DIY SEED-STARTING MIX & HOMEMADE SEED TRAYS

Once you have acquired your seeds, the next step is giving them the best possible start. While store-bought seed-starting mixes and trays can be expensive, you can create your own high-quality, nutrient-rich mix and containers at little to no cost.

1. Why Make Your Own Seed-Starting Mix?

Commercial seed-starting mixes are convenient, but they are often overpriced and may contain synthetic fertilizers or unnecessary additives. A DIY mix allows you to control ingredients, ensuring better seedling health while saving money.

A good seed-starting mix should be:

- **Lightweight and well-draining** – To prevent seed rot.
- **Moisture-retentive** – Seeds need consistent moisture to germinate.
- **Nutrient-balanced** – While seeds contain their own initial nutrients, a mild nutrient boost helps early growth.

2. Recipe for a DIY Seed-Starting Mix

This simple recipe mimics high-quality commercial seed-starting blends:

Basic DIY Seed-Starting Mix

- **1 part coconut coir or peat moss** – Retains moisture and keeps the mix light.
- **1 part perlite or sand** – Ensures drainage and aeration.
- **1 part compost or worm castings** – Provides slow-release nutrients.

For an extra boost, add:

- **A pinch of mycorrhizal fungi** – Supports root growth.
- **Crushed eggshells or wood ash** – Adds calcium to prevent deficiencies.

Mix all ingredients thoroughly and moisten slightly before filling containers.

3. Creating Homemade Seed Trays

Seed trays provide a contained space for seedlings to develop before transplanting. Instead of buying plastic trays, consider repurposing common household items.

Best Upcycled Seed-Starting Containers

- **Egg cartons** – Perfect for starting small seeds like lettuce or basil.
- **Toilet paper rolls** – Biodegradable and ideal for deep-rooted plants like beans.
- **Plastic clamshell containers** – (from berries or takeout) Create mini greenhouses by keeping the lid on.
- **Newspaper pots** – Rolled newspaper forms biodegradable cups that can be planted directly into the ground.

- **Yogurt cups & milk cartons** – Cut them down to size and poke drainage holes.

If using non-biodegradable containers, make sure to punch small holes at the bottom for drainage.

4. Labeling & Organization

To avoid confusion, label seed trays immediately after planting. Use:

- **Popsicle sticks or wooden spoons** – Write variety names with a waterproof marker.
- **Masking tape on containers** – Helps track dates and types of seeds.

Organizing trays in a warm, bright location ensures healthy germination. South-facing windows, heat mats, or simple shelf setups with LED lights can help seedlings grow strong before transplanting outdoors.

CHAPTER 2

FEBRUARY: SEED STARTING & SMART PURCHASES

February is the bridge between winter planning and spring action. This is the time to start seeds indoors, take advantage of budget-friendly gardening deals, and make strategic purchases that will pay off throughout the growing season. A cost-conscious gardener focuses on starting plants from seed rather than buying expensive transplants, sourcing quality supplies at the lowest cost, and making smart investments that enhance productivity without unnecessary spending.

By preparing now—organizing seeds, setting up a simple seed-starting system, and carefully selecting budget-friendly tools and amendments—you set the stage for a thriving, frugal garden in the months ahead.

WHEN TO BUY VS. WHEN TO DIY: COST-EFFECTIVE SEED STARTING SUPPLIES

Starting plants from seed is one of the smartest ways to save money in the garden. A single packet of seeds, often costing less than the price of one nursery-grown transplant, can produce dozens—or even hundreds—of plants. However, the costs of seed-starting supplies can add up quickly if you're not careful.

Many gardeners assume that a successful indoor seed-starting setup requires expensive grow lights, high-end seed trays, and specialty heating mats. While these tools have their place, there are countless ways to start seeds frugally using materials you may already have at home. The key is knowing when it's worth investing in quality supplies and when a DIY approach can deliver the same results for a fraction of the cost.

I learned this lesson through trial and error in my early gardening years. The first time I started seeds indoors, I fell into the common trap of overbuying. I was lured in by glossy catalogs and gardening stores filled with specialized seed-starting kits, premium soil mixes, and pricey humidity domes. My excitement led to a hefty bill, and while my seedlings thrived, I soon realized I could have achieved the same results with simple, low-cost alternatives.

The following season, determined to cut costs, I experimented with repurposed containers, homemade seedling mixes, and natural light sources. To my surprise, my plants were just as strong—if not stronger—than those I had pampered with expensive supplies. Over time, I developed a balanced approach: investing in a few high-value tools while embracing DIY solutions for the rest.

Below, we'll explore cost-effective seed-starting methods, breaking down which supplies are worth buying and where you can save money by making your own.

1. Seed Trays & Containers: Buy or Repurpose?

When to Buy:

- **If durability and reusability are priorities.** Investing in sturdy, reusable seed trays can be a wise long-term choice, as they last for years.
- **For uniform plant spacing and easier transplanting.** Standardized trays help seedlings grow evenly and reduce root disturbance when moving to the garden.

- **For high germination rates.** Quality trays often come with drainage holes and are designed to retain the right amount of moisture.

Recommended Purchase:

- Heavy-duty plastic seed trays with removable cells (reusable for years).
- Soil blocks (eliminate the need for plastic trays altogether).

When to DIY:

- **If you want to reduce waste and save money.** Many household items can be repurposed into seed-starting containers.
- **If you're growing a small number of plants.** There's no need to buy bulk trays if a handful of seedlings will suffice.

DIY Alternatives:

- Egg cartons (ideal for small seedlings but need careful watering).
- Yogurt cups or small food containers (poke holes for drainage).
- Toilet paper rolls (biodegradable, can be planted directly in the ground).
- Newspaper pots (easy to make, fully compostable).

Cost-Saving Tip: Many garden centers and nurseries discard used seed trays—ask if they have any available for free before purchasing new ones.

2. Seed-Starting Mix: Buy or Make Your Own?

When to Buy:

- **If you need a sterile, disease-free mix.** Store-bought seed-starting mixes are free of pathogens that could harm delicate seedlings.
- **If you're short on time.** Pre-mixed soil is ready to use immediately.
- **For consistency.** Commercial mixes are formulated for ideal moisture retention and aeration.

Recommended Purchase:

- Organic seed-starting mix with a fine texture (peat-free options are best for sustainability).

When to DIY:

- **If you want to cut costs significantly.** Making your own mix is cheaper than buying pre-made bags.
- **If you prefer sustainable alternatives.** Many commercial mixes rely on peat moss, which has environmental concerns.

DIY Seed-Starting Mix Recipe:

- **1 part compost (or sifted garden soil)** – Provides nutrients.
- **1 part coconut coir or peat moss** – Retains moisture.
- **1 part perlite or sand** – Improves drainage and aeration.

Cost-Saving Tip: Instead of perlite, use coarse sand or crushed eggshells for added aeration at no extra cost. we

3. Grow Lights & Natural Light: Invest or Improvise?

When to Buy:

- **If you start seeds in a dimly lit space.** Lack of sufficient light leads to weak, leggy seedlings.

- **For large-scale seed starting.** If growing dozens of seedlings, a proper grow light system is a good long-term investment.

Recommended Purchase:

- LED grow lights (energy-efficient, long-lasting, and produce minimal heat).
- Full-spectrum fluorescent shop lights (affordable and widely available).

When to DIY:

- **If you have access to bright windows.** South-facing windows can provide sufficient light for many seedlings.
- **If you can use natural reflectors.** Aluminum foil or white-painted cardboard can reflect light onto plants.
- **If you can rotate plants regularly.** Turning seed trays a few times a day helps prevent uneven growth.

Cost-Saving Tip: Instead of pricey grow lights, repurpose an old desk lamp with an LED bulb labeled "daylight" or "full spectrum."

4. Heating Mats & Germination Warmth: Necessary or Not?

When to Buy:

- **If growing heat-loving crops.** Peppers, tomatoes, and eggplants germinate better with consistent warmth.
- **If starting seeds in a cold basement or garage.** Heat mats provide reliable bottom warmth to speed up germination.

Recommended Purchase:

- A basic seedling heat mat with a thermostat for controlled temperatures.

When to DIY:

- **If growing cool-season crops.** Lettuce, kale, and many greens germinate well at room temperature.
- **If you have warm indoor spots.** Placing seed trays on top of a refrigerator or near a heating vent can provide gentle warmth.
- **If you can use insulation methods.** Placing trays inside a plastic storage bin with a lid can trap heat and moisture.

Cost-Saving Tip: Instead of a heating mat, fill a plastic bottle with warm water and place it in the seed tray overnight to maintain warmth.

5. Humidity Domes & Moisture Control: Buy or Improvise?

When to Buy:

- **If starting seeds in a dry climate.** Consistent humidity helps seeds germinate faster.
- **For convenience.** Pre-made humidity domes fit snugly over seed trays.

Recommended Purchase:

- Reusable plastic humidity domes or a greenhouse tray with a vented lid.

When to DIY:

- **If you have plastic covers at home.** Clear plastic lids from takeout containers work just as well.
- **If you want a biodegradable option.** Placing a damp paper towel over trays can maintain humidity temporarily.

Cost-Saving Tip: Repurpose clear plastic bakery containers or ziplock bags over small trays to create a humidity dome effect.

A Balanced Approach to Seed-Starting Costs

A successful, cost-effective seed-starting setup isn't about choosing between buying everything or DIYing everything—it's about striking the right balance. Some tools and supplies, like quality grow lights and durable seed trays, are long-term investments that can improve success and reduce costs over time. Others, like seed-starting containers, humidity domes, and even soil mixes, can be easily created from household materials at little to no cost.

BEST FRUGAL SOURCES FOR SOIL, COMPOST, AND AMENDMENTS

Soil is the foundation of a productive, cost-effective garden. Yet, many gardeners spend a fortune on bagged soil, synthetic fertilizers, and commercial compost—costs that add up quickly. The good news? Rich, healthy soil doesn't have to come from a store. With a strategic, frugal approach, you can build fertile ground using free or low-cost materials, many of which are readily available in your own backyard or community.

I learned this the hard way in my early gardening days. Eager to start a vegetable bed, I bought multiple bags of expensive garden soil, only to realize later that I could have sourced nearly everything for free. That experience led me to explore alternative methods—composting kitchen scraps, collecting fallen leaves, and even seeking out local farms for manure. The result? Not only did my soil improve dramatically, but my gardening expenses also dropped significantly.

Whether you're starting from scratch or enriching an existing garden, knowing where to source soil, compost, and amendments affordably can save hundreds of dollars over time.

1. Cost-Effective Ways to Get Quality Soil

Gardeners often assume they need to buy bagged soil to start a new bed, but nature already provides what's needed. If your native soil is poor, amending it is often cheaper than replacing it.

- **Sheet Mulching (Lasagna Gardening)** – Instead of hauling in soil, build it in place by layering cardboard, leaves, compost, and mulch. Over time, this breaks down into rich planting material.
- **Municipal Compost & Soil Programs** – Many cities offer free or low-cost compost, mulch, or topsoil to residents. Check with your local waste management or public works department.

- **Excavation Sites & Construction Projects** – Sometimes, landscapers or contractors have excess topsoil they are willing to give away. Be sure to ask about contamination risks.
- **Old Raised Beds & Garden Patches** – If you or a neighbor have an abandoned garden bed, the soil is often still viable. Revitalizing existing soil with compost is far cheaper than starting fresh.

2. Free or Low-Cost Sources of Compost

Compost is the lifeblood of a frugal garden. It enriches soil, reduces the need for store-bought fertilizers, and diverts waste from landfills—all at little to no cost.

- **Home Composting** – The most reliable and cost-effective method. Use food scraps, leaves, grass clippings, and shredded paper to create nutrient-rich compost.
- **Local Farms & Stables** – Many horse stables, dairy farms, and poultry farms give away manure for free. Aged manure makes an excellent compost base.
- **Coffee Shops & Restaurants** – Coffee grounds are a great nitrogen source and are often available for free from local cafés.
- **Tree Services & Landscaping Companies** – Some companies offer free wood chips, which break down into compost over time.
- **Community Compost Programs** – Some urban areas offer compost hubs where gardeners can pick up free finished compost.

3. Budget-Friendly Soil Amendments

Healthy soil needs a balance of nutrients, but that doesn't mean buying expensive fertilizers. Many natural amendments can be sourced inexpensively or even made at home.

- **Eggshells** – A free, natural source of calcium that helps prevent blossom-end rot in tomatoes and peppers.
- **Banana Peels** – Rich in potassium and phosphorus, these can be buried directly in the soil near plants.
- **Grass Clippings & Leaves** – Free, abundant, and an excellent way to add organic matter to garden beds.
- **Wood Ash** – A good source of potassium for alkaline-loving plants. Use sparingly to avoid altering soil pH too much.
- **Seaweed & Fish Scraps** – If you live near the coast, these are excellent mineral-rich amendments.

For larger-scale amendments, consider bartering with local farmers or joining community gardening groups to share bulk resources.

Building Fertile Soil on a Budget

Great soil doesn't come from expensive bags at the garden center—it comes from a gardener's resourcefulness. By composting at home, seeking out free local resources, and using natural amendments, you can build nutrient-rich soil without breaking the bank. The most productive gardens aren't the ones with the priciest inputs but the ones where the gardener understands how to work with nature, not against it.

CREATING A GARDEN LAYOUT TO MAXIMIZE SPACE & RESOURCES

A well-planned garden layout is one of the most powerful tools for saving money, increasing yields, and reducing labor. The way plants are arranged affects everything from sunlight exposure and airflow to soil fertility and water efficiency. By designing a layout that maximizes space and resources, a gardener can produce more food with less effort, fewer inputs, and minimal waste. The most productive gardens aren't necessarily the largest but rather the ones that make the best use of every square foot. Whether growing in a small backyard, a raised bed, or an expansive plot, strategic planning ensures that every plant thrives while reducing costs on water, soil amendments, and pest control.

1. Planning for Sunlight, Wind, and Water Efficiency

Before mapping out planting beds, it's important to analyze the natural conditions of the garden space. Sun-loving crops like tomatoes, peppers, and squash should be positioned where they receive at least 6–8 hours of direct sunlight, while leafy greens and root vegetables can tolerate partial shade. Wind protection is another key factor—strong winds can dry out soil and damage plants, so natural barriers like hedges, trellises, or taller companion plants help shield more delicate crops. Water flow and drainage should also be considered; drought-tolerant plants do well in higher or sloped areas, whereas moisture-loving crops thrive in low spots or near water catchment systems. Instead of relying heavily on irrigation, capturing rainwater through swales, barrels, or underground reservoirs makes watering more efficient and cost-effective.

2. Space-Saving Layout Techniques

Maximizing space means growing more food in less area while keeping plants healthy and productive. Square foot gardening, where crops are densely planted in small sections instead of traditional rows, reduces wasted space and helps control weeds. Interplanting and companion planting also maximize efficiency—for example, growing onions beside carrots saves space while naturally deterring pests. Vertical gardening is another effective technique, as trellises, cages, and stakes allow vining crops like cucumbers, beans, and peas to grow upward rather than outward, freeing up ground space for other plants. Additionally, succession planting ensures a continuous harvest by replanting quick-growing crops like lettuce, radishes, or herbs as soon as earlier crops are harvested. By layering these methods together, even the smallest garden can yield an abundant harvest.

3. Designing for Soil Health & Resource Conservation

A smart garden layout works with nature to improve soil health rather than depleting it. Raised beds and no-till gardening help retain moisture, encourage beneficial microbes, and reduce erosion, making the soil richer over time. Crop rotation prevents nutrient depletion and minimizes the buildup of pests and diseases, reducing the need for fertilizers and chemical treatments. Mulching with straw, wood chips, or grass clippings helps conserve moisture, suppress weeds, and improve soil structure, further cutting down on maintenance and external inputs. By focusing on long-term soil health, gardeners can build fertility naturally instead of relying on costly amendments.

4. Smart Pathways & Accessibility

A productive garden isn't just about planting—it's also about ease of movement and maintenance. Designing narrow paths while maximizing bed space ensures more growing area without wasted ground. Low-maintenance perennials or deep-rooted crops can be placed in harder-to-reach spots, while frequently harvested plants like herbs and salad greens should be positioned closer to walkways for easy access. Grouping plants with similar water needs together simplifies irrigation and prevents over- or under-watering. By designing with accessibility in mind, a well-laid-out garden becomes more efficient, requiring less effort to maintain while delivering maximum productivity.

A Thoughtful Layout Saves Time & Money

A smart garden layout is not just about fitting as many plants as possible into a space—it's about ensuring that each plant thrives while conserving resources. By planning for sunlight, airflow, soil health, and space efficiency, a gardener can reduce costs on water, fertilizers, and pest control while producing a bountiful harvest. The most successful gardens aren't the ones with the most space, but the ones where every square foot is used wisely.

WINTER SOWING: THE ULTRA-CHEAP COLD STRATIFICATION METHOD

Starting seeds early is one of the best ways to save money in the garden, but traditional indoor seed-starting setups can be expensive. Grow lights, heat mats, and seed trays all add up, and even with careful management, seedlings can become leggy or fail to thrive due to lack of natural conditions. That's where **winter sowing** comes in—a low-cost, low-maintenance method that harnesses the natural cold stratification process to produce strong, hardy seedlings without expensive equipment.

The first time I tried winter sowing, I was skeptical. The idea of planting seeds in the dead of winter and leaving them outside in milk jugs seemed absurd. But after years of struggling with fragile, indoor-started seedlings, I was willing to experiment. That spring, I was amazed—when the time was right, my seeds germinated on their own, and the seedlings were stocky, strong, and ready for transplanting. Since then, winter sowing has become my go-to method for starting cold-hardy plants at a fraction of the cost.

1. How Winter Sowing Works

Winter sowing mimics nature's process of cold stratification, which many seeds require to break dormancy. In their natural environment, seeds from plants like milkweed, spinach, lettuce, and many perennials fall to the ground in autumn, experience the chill of winter, and germinate when temperatures rise in spring. By recreating this cycle in homemade mini-greenhouses, gardeners can start seeds months earlier than direct sowing while avoiding the expense of indoor setups.

This method involves planting seeds in clear or translucent plastic containers—such as milk jugs, takeout containers, or soda bottles—that act as mini cold frames. These containers are left outside in the snow, rain, and fluctuating temperatures, allowing seeds to go through the natural freeze-thaw cycles they need. When spring arrives, the seeds sprout at the perfect time, having already adapted to outdoor conditions.

2. The Cost-Effectiveness of Winter Sowing

Unlike traditional seed-starting, winter sowing requires no expensive trays, potting mix, or artificial lighting. Almost everything needed can be repurposed for free. Milk jugs, soda bottles, and clear food containers make excellent mini-greenhouses, while leftover garden soil or compost provides a suitable growing medium. Since seedlings start outdoors, there's no need for heating mats or grow lights, cutting electricity costs and eliminating the stress of hardening off seedlings later.

Additionally, because winter-sown seedlings experience natural conditions from the start, they are stronger and less prone to transplant shock than greenhouse-grown seedlings. This reduces losses and ensures more plants survive to maturity—maximizing the value of every packet of seeds.

3. Best Plants for Winter Sowing

Not all seeds are suited to winter sowing, but many cold-hardy vegetables, herbs, and flowers thrive with this method. Leafy greens like kale, lettuce, and spinach are excellent candidates, as are root crops like beets and carrots. Hardy herbs such as parsley, chives, and cilantro germinate reliably, while perennial flowers like echinacea, rudbeckia, and milkweed benefit from cold stratification. Many native plants and wildflowers also respond well to this method, making winter sowing an affordable way to establish a pollinator-friendly garden.

For warm-season crops like tomatoes and peppers, winter sowing can still work, but these should be started later in the season, around late winter or early spring, to prevent premature sprouting during unexpected warm spells.

4. Step-by-Step Guide to Winter Sowing

1. **Prepare the Containers** – Cut milk jugs or plastic bottles in half, leaving a small hinge to keep the top attached. Poke drainage holes in the bottom to prevent waterlogging.
2. **Fill with Soil** – Use a few inches of well-draining soil or compost. Since these seeds will experience freezing and thawing, a heavy, moisture-retentive mix isn't necessary.
3. **Plant the Seeds** – Sow seeds at the recommended depth, water thoroughly, and replace the top of the container, securing it with duct tape. Remove the cap to allow ventilation.
4. **Place Outside** – Set the containers in a sunny, protected area where they will be exposed to rain and snow but not harsh winds.

5. **Let Nature Do the Work** – Over winter, the seeds will remain dormant, gradually experiencing the conditions they need for germination. When the weather warms, seedlings will emerge naturally.

Once seedlings outgrow their containers and outdoor temperatures stabilize, they can be transplanted directly into the garden—already acclimated to the elements, eliminating the need for a lengthy hardening-off process.

A No-Fuss, Ultra-Frugal Seed-Starting Method

Winter sowing is one of the simplest and most cost-effective ways to start a garden. It eliminates the need for expensive seed-starting supplies, produces hardy seedlings that require less care, and takes advantage of nature's own stratification process. For frugal gardeners, this method is a game-changer, proving that with a little creativity, great gardens can be grown for next to nothing.

PLANNING SUCCESSION PLANTING FOR CONTINUOUS HARVESTS & BLOOMS

A productive and visually stunning garden isn't just about a single, overwhelming harvest or a short-lived display of flowers—it's about continuous abundance. **Succession planting** is the key to maintaining a steady supply of vegetables, herbs, and flowers throughout the growing season. By staggering plantings, replacing spent plants with new ones, and incorporating fast-maturing varieties, gardeners can keep their beds full, ensuring they never experience a gap in production.

Traditional gardening often follows a single planting schedule, leading to cycles of excess followed by scarcity. Lettuce and spinach might mature all at once, causing waste, while flowers bloom briefly and then fade, leaving bare spaces. By contrast, succession planting spaces out plantings in intervals, ensuring a steady stream of vegetables and flowers while maximizing every inch of soil.

1. The Core Methods of Succession Planting

There are several ways to approach succession planting, each suited to different types of crops and flowers:

- **Staggered Planting (Timed Intervals):** Crops and flowers with a short maturity period—such as lettuce, radishes, zinnias, and cosmos—are sown in small batches every two to three weeks. This prevents overproduction and ensures a continuous harvest and bloom cycle.
- **Relay Planting (Replacing Crops as They Finish):** As one crop reaches maturity, another is immediately planted in its place. For instance, spring peas can be followed by summer beans, and later by fall spinach. For flowers, early tulips or daffodils can be followed by warm-season annuals like marigolds or celosia.
- **Multi-Season Planning (Spring, Summer, and Fall Successions):** Growing cool-season crops in early spring and late fall, with heat-loving crops in between, extends the harvest window. Likewise, planting early bloomers like daffodils and crocuses, followed by summer perennials like echinacea, and finishing with fall asters ensures flowers all season long.
- **Interplanting (Layering Crops & Flowers Together):** Fast-growing crops like radishes can be sown alongside slower-maturing ones like carrots. Similarly, flowers such as alyssum or nasturtiums can be planted between vegetables to attract pollinators while maximizing space.

2. Best Plants for Succession Planting

Not all plants are suited for succession planting, but many vegetables, herbs, and flowers thrive with careful scheduling.

Vegetables & Herbs

Fast-growing vegetables like lettuce, spinach, radishes, bush beans, and green onions are perfect for staggered sowing. **Cool-season crops** such as carrots, beets, and kale can be planted in multiple waves—once in early spring, again in midsummer for fall harvest, and sometimes even late fall for overwintering. **Warm-season crops** like cucumbers, summer squash, and basil benefit from being replanted mid-season to maintain a fresh, productive supply.

Flowers

Annual flowers like **zinnias, cosmos, sunflowers, and marigolds** bloom quickly and benefit from successive plantings to keep beds colorful throughout the season. **Biennials and perennials** like foxglove, echinacea, and rudbeckia can be planted strategically to ensure waves of blooms at different times. For continuous floral displays, gardeners can plan for spring bulbs (tulips, daffodils), followed by summer blooms (black-eyed Susans, coreopsis), and finally late-season stars like chrysanthemums and asters.

Zinnias

3. Creating a Succession Planting Schedule

A successful succession planting plan starts with understanding the **first and last frost dates** and the **days to maturity** for each crop or flower. Using a planting calendar helps ensure that as one plant finishes, another is ready to take its place.

For example, in a 120-day growing season:

- **Lettuce & Spinach** can be sown every two weeks from early spring until mid-fall.
- **Bush Beans & Zinnias** can be planted every three weeks for continuous production.
- **Carrots & Beets** can be sown in early spring and again in late summer for a fall crop.

- **Sunflowers & Cosmos** can be replanted mid-summer to maintain fresh blooms into autumn.

4. Maximizing Space & Resources with Smart Transitions

To make the most of limited space, every planting transition should be efficient. Raised beds or containers, which warm up quickly, allow for earlier plantings and faster crop turnover. **Pre-starting seedlings** indoors or in a protected area ensures that new plants are ready to go as soon as space opens up in the garden.

Additionally, cover crops like **clover or buckwheat** can be planted between vegetable successions to improve soil fertility, prevent weeds, and add nutrients. For flowers, mixing short-lived annuals with longer-lasting perennials ensures continuous color without needing constant replanting.

A Garden That Never Stops Producing

With careful planning, succession planting transforms a garden into a space of continuous abundance—whether it's fresh vegetables and herbs for the kitchen or waves of flowers for beauty and pollinators. By staggering plantings, rotating crops and blooms efficiently, and making use of every growing opportunity, gardeners can create a thriving, productive landscape that remains full and flourishing from spring to fall. With smart scheduling, a small garden can provide both a steady food supply and an ever-changing floral display, proving that thoughtful planting leads to lasting rewards.

CHAPTER 3

MARCH: MAXIMIZING FREE RESOURCES

As winter fades and the garden begins to wake up, March is the perfect time to gather and utilize free or low-cost resources to enrich the soil, expand plantings, and prepare for the growing season ahead. Smart gardeners know that a thriving garden doesn't have to come with a hefty price tag—nature provides many of the materials needed to build fertility, support plant health, and maximize productivity. From collecting leaves and composting kitchen scraps to sourcing free mulch, cuttings, and seeds, this month focuses on resourcefulness and sustainability. By tapping into what's readily available—whether through nature, community networks, or repurposed materials—you can cultivate abundance without breaking the bank.

THE BEST FREE SOIL AMENDMENTS

Healthy, fertile soil is the foundation of a productive garden, yet many gardeners spend a small fortune on commercial fertilizers and amendments. The truth is, some of the best soil enhancers are completely free, readily available in nature, or can be repurposed from household and garden waste. By using locally sourced, organic materials, gardeners can improve soil structure, boost nutrient levels, and create a thriving ecosystem—all without spending a dime.

In one community garden, an elderly gardener named Mr. Thomas was famous for growing the healthiest vegetables, yet he never bought commercial fertilizers. His secret? A deep understanding of how to work with nature's resources. He used everything from fallen leaves to coffee grounds, turning what others discarded into a soil-building goldmine. His methods proved that with a little creativity, free amendments can be just as effective—if not better—than store-bought options.

1. Leaf Mold: Nature's Perfect Soil Conditioner

Every autumn, millions of leaves fall, and most people bag them up for disposal—but for frugal gardeners, leaves are an invaluable resource. When left to decompose, they break down into a rich, crumbly substance called leaf mold, which improves soil aeration, water retention, and microbial life.

Leaf mold

How to Make Leaf Mold for Free:

1. Gather leaves in the fall (oak, maple, and beech are excellent choices).
2. Store them in a pile, compost bin, or perforated garbage bags.

3. Keep them moist and allow them to break down over several months to a year.

2. Grass Clippings: A Nitrogen Powerhouse

Fresh grass clippings are a fantastic source of nitrogen, an essential nutrient for plant growth. Instead of throwing them away, they can be used as mulch or a compost booster. However, clippings should be applied in thin layers to prevent matting and anaerobic decay.

How to Use Grass Clippings in the Garden:

- **Mulch:** Spread a thin layer around plants to suppress weeds and retain moisture.
- **Compost Accelerator:** Mix with carbon-rich materials like dried leaves or shredded paper to speed up decomposition.

When used correctly, grass clippings feed the soil and reduce the need for synthetic fertilizers.

3. Coffee Grounds: A Slow-Release Fertilizer

Many coffee shops offer free used coffee grounds to gardeners because they would otherwise be thrown away. Rich in nitrogen, phosphorus, and potassium, coffee grounds act as a slow-release organic fertilizer. They also improve soil texture and attract earthworms, which naturally aerate the soil.

Ways to Use Coffee Grounds for Free:

- Sprinkle around plants to provide a slow-release nutrient boost.
- Add to compost bins to enhance decomposition.
- Mix with mulch to repel slugs and snails.

A librarian-turned-gardener in Seattle once transformed her depleted backyard soil using nothing but free coffee grounds from a local café. Within a year, her garden—once barren—was bursting with deep-green kale and tomatoes, all thanks to this simple, cost-free amendment.

Coffee grounds

4. Wood Ash: A Natural pH Balancer

For gardeners with acidic soil, wood ash from untreated fireplaces or bonfires can be a game-changer. It contains potassium, calcium, and trace minerals, helping to neutralize overly acidic conditions.

How to Use Wood Ash Safely:

- **Sprinkle lightly** in garden beds (excess can raise soil pH too much).

- Use around fruit trees, tomatoes, and brassicas to provide potassium.
- Avoid applying near acid-loving plants like blueberries and rhododendrons.

By applying wood ash in moderation, gardeners can naturally balance soil pH without expensive lime amendments.

5. Manure: A Time-Tested Soil Booster

Farmers have used animal manure for centuries to build soil fertility. **Cow, horse, rabbit, and chicken manure** are excellent sources of organic matter, rich in nitrogen and beneficial microbes. Many small farms or stables offer it for free—especially if gardeners are willing to haul it themselves.

Best Practices for Using Manure:

- **Compost before use** (fresh manure can be too strong and may burn plants).
- Mix with straw or leaves to balance nutrients.
- Apply in fall or early spring to enrich soil before planting.

With proper composting, manure becomes a nutrient-rich, cost-free amendment that improves soil structure and plant health.

Abundant Soil Fertility Without the Cost

Building healthy soil doesn't require store-bought fertilizers. By tapping into natural, free amendments like leaf mold, grass clippings, coffee grounds, wood ash, and manure, gardeners can enrich their soil sustainably. These time-tested, cost-free resources feed the earth while reducing waste, proving that the best solutions often come from working with nature—not against it.

THE POWER OF COMPOSTING: MAKING "BLACK GOLD" FOR FREE

Composting is one of the most valuable skills a frugal gardener can master. By recycling kitchen scraps, garden waste, and organic materials, composting creates a nutrient-rich soil amendment that improves plant health, boosts soil fertility, and eliminates the need for chemical fertilizers.

A small-town community garden once struggled with poor soil and declining yields. Instead of buying expensive amendments, they launched a composting initiative—encouraging members to bring food scraps, leaves, and garden waste. Within two years, the garden's productivity skyrocketed, all thanks to homemade compost, affectionately called "black gold."

1. What Makes Compost So Powerful?

Compost is more than just decomposed organic matter—it's a living ecosystem teeming with beneficial microbes. These microbes break down nutrients into forms that plants can absorb, enriching soil without synthetic fertilizers. Compost also:

- **Improves soil structure**, making clay soil looser and sandy soil more moisture-retentive.
- **Boosts microbial life**, supporting earthworms and beneficial bacteria.
- **Balances soil nutrients**, preventing deficiencies that hinder plant growth.

2. How to Start Composting for Free

Starting a compost pile is simple and requires no special equipment. It follows a basic ratio of **green (nitrogen-rich) and brown (carbon-rich) materials**:

Greens (Nitrogen-Rich, Moist Materials)

- Fruit and vegetable scraps
- Coffee grounds
- Grass clippings
- Manure (from herbivores)

Browns (Carbon-Rich, Dry Materials)

- Leaves
- Shredded cardboard/newspaper
- Wood chips
- Straw

Step-by-Step Guide to Making Compost:

1. **Choose a Location** – A shaded spot with good drainage works best.
2. **Layer Greens & Browns** – Aim for a **balanced mix** to speed up decomposition.
3. **Keep it Moist** – Like a wrung-out sponge, compost should be damp but not soggy.
4. **Turn Occasionally** – Stir the pile to aerate it and accelerate breakdown.
5. **Harvest When Ready** – Finished compost is dark, crumbly, and smells like fresh earth.

3. Composting Without a Pile: Free & Simple Methods

Not everyone has space for a large compost pile, but there are alternatives:

- **Trench Composting** – Dig a hole, bury food scraps, and let them break down directly in garden beds.
- **Sheet Mulching (Lasagna Gardening)** – Layer compostable materials directly on garden soil, letting nature do the work.
- **Worm Composting (Vermicomposting)** – A great method for small spaces, using red worms to break down food scraps into rich castings.

TURNING WASTE INTO GARDEN GOLD

Composting transforms everyday waste into one of the most valuable garden resources—for free. Whether using a traditional compost pile, trench composting, or worm bins, the result is the same: nutrient-dense, organic matter that nourishes the soil and supports plant growth. For the resourceful gardener, composting is not just a technique—it's a powerful, sustainable way to cultivate abundance without spending a penny.

Gardening offers numerous benefits, from providing fresh produce to enhancing mental well-being. However, the associated costs can be a concern for many. By adopting budget-friendly practices, gardeners can cultivate thriving spaces without significant financial investment. This guide delves into three effective strategies: utilizing affordable mulching materials, sourcing free or low-cost plants, and constructing DIY greenhouses from salvaged materials.

MULCHING ON A BUDGET

Mulching is a vital gardening practice that helps conserve soil moisture, suppress weeds, and enrich soil fertility. Fortunately, effective mulching doesn't require expensive materials. Common household and yard waste can serve as excellent, cost-free mulch options.

Grass Clippings: After mowing, instead of discarding grass clippings, consider using them as mulch. They provide a nitrogen boost to the soil and decompose quickly. It's essential to apply a thin layer to prevent matting and potential mold growth. Allowing the clippings to dry slightly before application can also help in preventing odor issues. citeturn0search10

Shredded Paper: Recycling paper from home or local businesses can serve as an effective mulch. Shredded newspaper or office paper helps retain soil moisture and suppress weeds. Ensure the paper is free from glossy inks and apply it in combination with other organic materials to prevent it from blowing away. This method not only benefits the garden but also reduces household waste. citeturn0search4

Wood Chips: Local tree services often have an excess of wood chips from pruning activities. These can be acquired at little to no cost and make for durable mulch that breaks down slowly, enriching the soil over time. It's advisable to let fresh wood chips age for a few months before use to avoid potential nitrogen depletion in the soil.

In a suburban community garden, members collaborated with a local tree trimming service to obtain free wood chips. This initiative not only conserved soil moisture but also fostered a partnership within the community, demonstrating the benefits of resourcefulness and collaboration.

FINDING FREE OR LOW-COST PLANTS

Expanding a garden doesn't have to strain your budget. Numerous avenues exist to acquire plants affordably or even for free.

Plant Sales and Swaps: Many horticultural societies and community groups host annual plant sales or swaps. These events offer a variety of plants at reduced prices or even for free. Attending these events not only provides access to affordable plants but also offers opportunities to connect with fellow gardening enthusiasts.

Online Communities: Platforms like Freecycle or local gardening forums often have members looking to share surplus plants or seeds. Engaging with these communities can lead to discovering new plant varieties without any cost. For instance, the Facebook group "Free plants and seeds for humanity" is dedicated to sharing surplus plants, cuttings, and seeds among members. citeturn0search1

Friends and Neighbors: Sharing plant cuttings or divisions is a common practice among gardeners. A simple conversation with a neighbor might result in exchanging plant varieties, benefiting both parties. This method not only diversifies your garden but also strengthens community bonds.

In one neighborhood, a group of gardeners organized a plant swap event every spring. Participants brought surplus seedlings and cuttings, fostering a sense of community while diversifying their gardens without spending money.

DIY GREENHOUSE IDEAS FROM SALVAGED MATERIALS

Constructing a greenhouse can extend your growing season and protect plants from adverse weather. Building one from salvaged materials makes it both eco-friendly and economical.

Reclaimed Windows and Doors: Old windows and doors can be repurposed to create the walls and roof of a greenhouse, providing ample light and insulation. This approach not only reduces waste but also adds a unique aesthetic to your garden.

Pallets and Scrap Wood: Wooden pallets and scrap lumber can form the framework of the structure. Ensure the wood is untreated to avoid introducing chemicals into your garden. Pallets are often available for free from businesses looking to dispose of them, making them a cost-effective building material.

My Greenhouse from 100% salvage material

Plastic Bottles: Collecting and stacking plastic bottles can create insulating walls that allow light to penetrate while maintaining internal temperatures. This method is an excellent way to recycle plastic waste and is particularly suitable for small-scale greenhouse projects.

A gardening enthusiast constructed a greenhouse using discarded windows collected from renovation sites. This not only diverted waste from landfills but also provided a functional and charming greenhouse that became the centerpiece of their garden.

CHAPTER 4

APRIL: SMART PLANTING & WASTE REDUCTION

April marks a pivotal time in the gardening calendar, presenting an ideal opportunity to implement strategies that promote both plant health and environmental stewardship. The chapter "April: Smart Planting & Waste Reduction" delves into practices that not only enhance garden productivity but also minimize ecological impact. Key topics include efficient planting techniques tailored to the spring season and methods to reduce waste through sustainable gardening practices. By adopting these approaches, gardeners can foster a more resilient and eco-friendly garden environment.

DIRECT SOWING VS. TRANSPLANTING: SAVING MONEY WITH THE RIGHT APPROACH

In the realm of gardening, the choice between direct sowing and transplanting significantly influences plant health, labor investment, and financial outlay. Understanding the nuances of each method enables gardeners to make informed decisions that align with their goals and resources.

Direct Sowing involves planting seeds directly into the garden soil where they will mature. This approach is often favored for its simplicity and cost-effectiveness. Gardeners bypass the need for indoor seed-starting setups, thereby reducing expenses associated with pots, soil mixes, and grow lights. Additionally, plants grown from direct sowing typically develop robust root systems, as they remain undisturbed throughout their growth. However, this method can be seed-intensive due to potential losses from environmental factors, necessitating practices like thinning to ensure optimal plant spacing.

Conversely, **Transplanting** entails starting seeds indoors or in controlled environments before relocating seedlings to the garden. This technique offers a head start on the growing season, which is particularly advantageous in regions with shorter warm periods. Transplanting can lead to earlier harvests and may enhance yields for certain crops. Nevertheless, it requires an initial investment in equipment and supplies, and the process demands careful management to prevent transplant shock, which can impede plant development.

A study by Westar Seeds highlights that while transplanting incurs higher initial costs due to indoor cultivation and transplantation efforts, it can result in savings on seed usage, weeding, and irrigation. The choice between direct seeding and transplanting often balances out in terms of cost and yield, depending on a grower's specific circumstances. citeturn0search1

An illustrative example comes from a community garden in the Midwest, where gardeners experimented with both methods for their tomato crops. Those who started seeds indoors and transplanted seedlings reported earlier fruiting and higher overall yields. In contrast, gardeners who direct-sowed tomato seeds faced challenges with germination rates and later harvests. This experience underscored the benefits of transplanting for certain crops in regions with shorter growing seasons.

In summary, the decision between direct sowing and transplanting hinges on various factors, including crop type, climate conditions, available resources, and specific gardening objectives. By carefully evaluating these elements, gardeners can select the method that best aligns with their needs, optimizing both plant health and economic efficiency.

HOW TO GROW YOUR OWN MULCH AND FERTILIZER

Cultivating your own mulch and fertilizer is a sustainable and cost-effective approach to enriching your garden's soil. By growing specific plants known for their soil-enhancing properties, you can create a self-sustaining ecosystem that reduces reliance on external inputs.

Comfrey is a prime example of a plant that serves dual purposes in the garden. Its deep taproots draw nutrients from the subsoil, storing them in its large, nutrient-rich leaves. By periodically cutting back comfrey foliage and applying it as a mulch around other plants, gardeners can naturally fertilize their soil. This practice not only suppresses weeds but also enriches the soil as the leaves decompose. In a community garden in Oregon, members planted comfrey alongside their vegetable plots. Throughout the growing season, they harvested the leaves to mulch their crops, resulting in noticeable improvements in plant health and yield.

Clover, particularly red and white varieties, is another valuable plant for soil enhancement. As a legume, clover has the unique ability to fix atmospheric nitrogen into the soil through a symbiotic relationship with root-dwelling bacteria. Planting clover as a cover crop or between rows in a vegetable garden can improve soil fertility and structure. For instance, a small-scale farmer in Iowa integrated white clover into her crop rotation. After the main harvest, she sowed clover seeds, which grew during the off-season. Before planting the next crop, she tilled the clover into the soil, providing a natural nitrogen boost and enhancing soil organic matter.

The concept of **dynamic accumulators** involves plants that are believed to absorb and store higher concentrations of specific nutrients from the soil. When these plants are composted or used as mulch, they can release these nutrients back into the soil, making them available to other plants. While the scientific community continues to study the efficacy of dynamic accumulators, many gardeners have found success using plants like **nettles** and **borage** in this capacity. In a permaculture garden in the United Kingdom, the gardener allowed nettles to grow in designated areas. Once mature, he harvested them to create a nutrient-rich compost tea, which he used to fertilize his fruiting plants, observing increased vigor and productivity.

By intentionally cultivating these beneficial plants, gardeners can create a regenerative system that produces its own mulch and fertilizer. This approach not only reduces costs associated with purchasing external inputs but also promotes a healthier, more resilient garden ecosystem. Embracing these practices fosters a deeper connection to the natural cycles of growth and decay, leading to a more sustainable and rewarding gardening experience.

FREE WATER SOURCES & RAINWATER COLLECTION SYSTEMS

Harnessing free water sources and implementing rainwater collection systems are effective strategies for sustainable gardening, reducing reliance on municipal water supplies and promoting environmental stewardship.

Rainwater Harvesting

Collecting rainwater is a practical method to utilize natural precipitation for garden irrigation. A common approach involves directing rainwater from rooftops into storage containers. For instance, installing gutters and downspouts on your home or garden shed can channel rainwater into barrels or tanks. Ensuring these collection points are equipped with screens or filters helps prevent debris and insects from contaminating the water. This harvested rainwater can then be used during dry periods, providing a readily available and cost-free irrigation source. citeturn0search3

In a practical example, a gardener in Atlanta utilized a 400-gallon IBC container placed in his basement to collect rainwater. By connecting a pump to this system, he efficiently supplied water to his garden's drip irrigation network, significantly reducing his dependence on city water. citeturn0search7

Greywater Reuse

Another valuable free water source is greywater, which includes water from sinks, showers, and washing machines, excluding toilet waste. By repurposing greywater for garden use, you can conserve fresh water and reduce utility costs. It's essential to use biodegradable, plant-friendly soaps and detergents to prevent soil contamination. Implementing a greywater system can range from simple bucket collection methods to more complex plumbing installations that divert greywater directly to garden areas. In Melbourne, a homeowner named Alan Leenaerts effectively used greywater to sustain his rainwater tanks, benefiting his garden and promoting water conservation. citeturn0news19

Alternative Water Sources

Exploring other free water sources can further enhance your garden's sustainability. For example, if your property has access to a pond, well, or natural waterway, these can serve as irrigation sources, provided appropriate water rights and environmental considerations are observed. Additionally, implementing rain gardens—designed to capture and filter runoff from impervious surfaces like driveways—can help manage water flow and provide moisture to garden plants. citeturn0search0turn0search17

Embracing sustainability in gardening involves creatively repurposing household waste into functional tools and supports, as well as extending the life of seedlings through upcycling. These practices not only reduce environmental impact but also offer cost-effective solutions for gardeners.

REPURPOSING HOUSEHOLD WASTE INTO GARDEN TOOLS AND PLANT SUPPORTS

Many everyday items destined for the trash can find new life in the garden. For instance, plastic jugs can be transformed into mini-greenhouses to protect young plants. By cutting a hole into the handle and securing the jug with a bamboo stake, gardeners can prevent it from being dislodged by wind. citeturn0search0

Old metal hanging planters can be repurposed into hanging "balls" by wiring two together, providing unique structures for climbing plants or decorative elements in the garden. citeturn0search2

Additionally, worn-out towels can be cut into strips and used as soft plant ties, offering gentle support to growing stems without causing damage. citeturn0news22

EXTENDING THE LIFE OF SEEDLINGS THROUGH UPCYCLING

Starting seeds in upcycled containers is an eco-friendly way to nurture young plants. Cardboard egg cartons, for example, serve as biodegradable seed starters. Once seedlings are ready for transplanting, the individual sections can be planted directly into the soil, reducing transplant shock and waste. citeturn0search7

Plastic cell packs from previous plant purchases can be washed and reused for multiple seasons. By sowing seeds in these recycled packs, gardeners can organize different plant varieties efficiently. citeturn0search5

Containers like yogurt cups or plastic bottles can also be repurposed as seedling pots. By ensuring proper drainage holes are added, these items provide suitable environments for young plants to develop before being transplanted into the garden. citeturn0search3

CHAPTER 5

MAY: GROWING FOOD FOR FREE (OR ALMOST FREE)

In May, our focus shifts to the empowering practice of cultivating your own food with minimal financial investment. By leveraging sustainable gardening techniques, repurposing household items, and engaging with community resources, it's possible to grow a variety of fruits, vegetables, and herbs at little to no cost. This approach not only promotes self-sufficiency but also fosters a deeper connection to the food we consume, all while contributing to environmental sustainability.

PERENNIAL EDIBLES: INVEST ONCE, HARVEST FOR YEARS

Investing in perennial edibles offers gardeners the advantage of planting once and harvesting for many years. These long-lived plants not only provide a consistent supply of food but also contribute to a sustainable and low-maintenance gardening approach.

Benefits of Growing Perennial Edibles

1. **Reduced Labor and Maintenance**: Perennials establish deep root systems, making them more resilient to drought and less dependent on frequent watering. Once established, they often require less care compared to annuals, as they can outcompete weeds and are less susceptible to pests. citeturn0search3
2. **Soil Health Improvement**: The extensive root systems of perennials enhance soil structure and fertility. As these roots grow and decompose over time, they add organic matter to the soil, improving its structure and nutrient content. citeturn0search1

3. **Environmental Sustainability**: By reducing the need for replanting and minimizing soil disturbance, perennials help maintain soil integrity and reduce erosion. Their longevity also means fewer resources are needed for planting and cultivation. citeturn0search6

Examples of Perennial Edibles

- **Asparagus**: A spring favorite, asparagus can produce spears for up to 20 years once established. It thrives in well-drained soils and benefits from full sun exposure.
- **Rhubarb**: Known for its tart stalks, rhubarb is a hardy perennial that can be harvested annually. It's well-suited to cooler climates and requires minimal maintenance.
- **Jerusalem Artichoke (Sunchoke)**: This tuberous sunflower relative produces edible tubers that can be harvested in the fall. It's adaptable to various soil types and can become a reliable food source.
- **Perennial Kale**: Unlike its annual counterparts, perennial kale varieties can provide greens year-round in milder climates. They are resilient and can withstand light frosts.

Incorporating Perennials into Your Garden

When planning a garden, consider integrating perennial edibles alongside annual crops. This combination ensures a continuous harvest and diversifies the garden's productivity. Perennials can serve as foundational plants, creating a stable structure around which annuals can be rotated.

For instance, a gardener in the Pacific Northwest established a bed of asparagus and rhubarb along the northern edge of their garden. These perennials provided early spring harvests, allowing the gardener to focus on planting annual vegetables in other areas as the season progressed.

In tropical regions, plants like moringa and perennial spinaches (e.g., Malabar spinach) offer nutritious leaves year-round. A community garden in Florida incorporated moringa trees, benefiting from their rapid growth and edible leaves, which are rich in vitamins and minerals.

THE EASIEST PLANTS TO GROW FROM KITCHEN SCRAPS

Regrowing plants from kitchen scraps is one of the most rewarding, cost-effective, and sustainable gardening techniques. It turns what would otherwise be waste into a continuous source of fresh food. With just a little effort, you can transform leftover vegetable scraps into thriving plants, reducing grocery costs and making the most of what you already have.

The Magic of Regrowing Food from Scraps

Many plants have a natural ability to regenerate, and some require nothing more than water and sunlight to begin sprouting again. This method of growing food is not only budget-friendly but also deeply satisfying. Imagine chopping green onions for a meal, placing the root ends in a cup of water, and watching them sprout new leaves within days. It's a process that feels almost magical yet is entirely rooted in science.

A schoolteacher once introduced this concept to her students by placing carrot tops in shallow dishes of water. Within a week, tiny green shoots began to emerge. The children were amazed, learning firsthand how plants can regenerate and how food scraps can be transformed into something new. This simple act planted the seed of sustainability in young minds.

Vegetables That Regrow with Minimal Effort

Green Onions, Leeks, and Garlic

One of the easiest and fastest crops to regrow from scraps is green onions. After using the leafy tops, the white roots can be placed in a glass of water on a sunny windowsill. Within a few days, fresh green shoots emerge, ready to be harvested again and again.

A home cook who enjoyed fresh green onions daily once planted them in a small pot on her kitchen counter. Every few days, she snipped what she needed, and the onions kept regenerating. What started as a single purchase from the grocery store turned into a nearly endless supply. The same process works for leeks and even garlic—planting a single clove can produce a whole new bulb over time.

Lettuce, Celery, and Bok Choy

Leafy greens like romaine lettuce, celery, and bok choy can regenerate from their base. By placing the trimmed end in a shallow dish of water, new leaves start to form within a week. Once the roots develop, the plant can be transferred into soil for continued growth.

One gardener in an urban apartment kept a small indoor "salad bar" by regrowing romaine lettuce and celery scraps. She found that even with limited space, she could have a steady supply of fresh greens simply by using what would otherwise be thrown away.

Potatoes and Sweet Potatoes

Sprouted potatoes are another excellent candidate for regrowth. If a potato has eyes (small growing points), it can be cut into chunks, with each piece containing at least one sprout. When planted in soil, these pieces will develop into full potato plants.

An elderly farmer recalled how his grandmother never wasted a sprouting potato. Instead of discarding it, she would plant it in a barrel filled with soil, adding more soil as the plant grew. By the end of the season, the barrel would be overflowing with fresh potatoes. The same technique works for sweet potatoes—allowing a sprouted tuber to develop shoots (or "slips") before planting them in the garden.

Carrots, Beets, and Turnips

Root vegetables like carrots, beets, and turnips won't regrow a full root from scraps, but they will produce fresh greens that are edible and nutritious. By placing the cut-off tops in shallow water, they quickly send up leafy greens that can be used in salads, soups, or sautés.

A permaculture enthusiast discovered this trick when experimenting with waste reduction. She found that not only could she regrow beet greens repeatedly, but they also made an excellent addition to compost when she was finished harvesting them.

Herbs Like Basil, Mint, and Cilantro

Many soft-stemmed herbs, such as basil, mint, and cilantro, can be regrown from cuttings. By placing a sprig in water, roots begin to form within a week. Once established, the cutting can be planted in soil for a continuous supply of fresh herbs.

One chef, frustrated by constantly buying fresh basil, started regrowing his own from supermarket leftovers. Within a month, he had enough basil to last him all season, simply by trimming and propagating cuttings from a single bunch.

From Scraps to Sustainability

Regrowing plants from kitchen scraps is more than just a clever gardening trick—it's a step toward a more sustainable lifestyle. It reduces waste, saves money, and provides fresh, homegrown food with minimal effort. Whether you're in a city apartment or a backyard homestead, these simple methods allow anyone to turn kitchen leftovers into a thriving garden. The joy of seeing new life emerge from scraps is a reminder that nature is endlessly generous, and with a little care, we can reap its rewards again and again.

COMPANION PLANTING FOR PEST CONTROL: REDUCING THE NEED FOR SPRAYS

Companion planting is one of the most effective and natural ways to control pests in the garden. By strategically growing certain plants together, gardeners can create a balanced ecosystem where beneficial insects thrive, harmful pests are deterred, and plants support each other's health. This approach eliminates or significantly reduces the need for chemical sprays, making it a cost-effective and environmentally friendly method of pest management.

The Wisdom of Nature: How Plants Protect Each Other

For centuries, gardeners and farmers have observed how certain plants grow better together, while others struggle when placed side by side. Some plants release natural compounds that repel pests, while others attract beneficial insects that keep harmful bugs in check.

Understanding these relationships allows gardeners to create a system where nature does most of the pest control work.

An organic farmer once shared how he struggled with aphids devouring his lettuce crop. Frustrated, he experimented with planting marigolds between the rows. To his amazement, the aphid problem diminished within weeks. The marigolds attracted ladybugs, which fed on the aphids, restoring balance without a single spray.

Plants That Repel Pests Naturally

Many plants emit strong scents or chemicals that deter common garden pests. By interplanting these among vegetables, gardeners can create a natural pest barrier.

- **Marigolds** are famous for repelling nematodes and aphids. Their strong scent confuses pests and prevents infestations.
- **Basil** planted near tomatoes not only enhances flavor but also repels mosquitoes and whiteflies.
- **Chives and onions** deter carrot flies, aphids, and Japanese beetles.
- **Rosemary and thyme** naturally repel cabbage worms and moths that attack brassicas.

A community gardener noticed that his cabbage plants, which were typically riddled with holes from cabbage worms, remained untouched when he surrounded them with rosemary. He never had to spray his greens again.

Trap Crops: Luring Pests Away

Another technique in companion planting involves using "trap crops" to attract pests away from more valuable plants.

- **Nasturtiums** draw aphids, keeping them off tomatoes, peppers, and beans.
- **Radishes** can be planted near squash to attract flea beetles away from the main crop.
- **Mustard greens** serve as a sacrificial crop for caterpillars, sparing cabbages and collards.

One homesteader shared how she planted nasturtiums at the edges of her garden and watched as aphids flocked to them instead of her vegetables. It was a small sacrifice that saved her harvest.

Attracting Beneficial Insects for Natural Pest Control

Not all bugs in the garden are bad. Ladybugs, lacewings, and hoverflies feast on aphids, while predatory wasps hunt caterpillars. Companion planting can help attract these garden allies.

- **Dill, fennel, and cilantro** produce tiny flowers that draw in lacewings and parasitic wasps.
- **Sunflowers** attract birds that eat caterpillars and beetles.
- **Yarrow and alyssum** provide nectar for pollinators and predatory insects.

A small-scale farmer once struggled with hornworms destroying his tomato crop. After planting dill and yarrow nearby, he noticed tiny wasps laying eggs on the caterpillars. The hornworms were soon gone, and his tomatoes thrived without any pesticides.

The Power of Diversity in the Garden

A monoculture—where only one type of crop is grown—invites pest infestations. Pests easily find their preferred plants when they are grown in large, uninterrupted blocks. By mixing different plants together, gardeners make it harder for pests to locate their targets.

A gardener who had dealt with squash vine borers year after year decided to plant her zucchini among sunflowers, basil, and nasturtiums instead of in a single row. That year, she had fewer borers than ever before. The diverse planting made it difficult for the pests to hone in on their usual target.

THE NO-COST WAY TO CREATE A SELF-SEEDING GARDEN

A self-seeding garden is one of nature's simplest and most rewarding gifts. With little effort and no cost, plants can drop their own seeds, germinate naturally, and return year after year—sometimes even surprising you by sprouting in unexpected places. By embracing self-seeding plants, gardeners can reduce labor, save money on seeds, and enjoy a thriving, low-maintenance garden that practically grows itself.

The Beauty of Letting Nature Take Over

Many gardeners are used to meticulously planting rows of seeds each season, but nature has a different approach. In the wild, plants bloom, produce seeds, and scatter them naturally—whether by wind, birds, or simply falling to the ground. Those seeds germinate at just the right time, following the rhythm of the seasons. By mimicking this process, gardeners can create a flourishing space that requires minimal replanting.

A homesteader once shared how she accidentally discovered the magic of self-seeding. One fall, she left a few arugula plants to flower and forgot about them. The following spring, to her delight, tiny arugula sprouts covered the garden bed. She hadn't sown a single seed that year, yet her salad greens were already growing—an effortless, no-cost harvest.

How to Encourage a Self-Seeding Garden

Choose Plants That Readily Reseed Themselves

Not all plants self-seed effectively, but many annuals, biennials, and even some perennials will readily drop seeds and return on their own. Some of the easiest vegetables, herbs, and flowers to encourage self-seeding include:

- **Vegetables:** Lettuce, arugula, kale, radishes, carrots, tomatoes, and squash
- **Herbs:** Cilantro, dill, basil, chives, and chamomile
- **Flowers:** Marigolds, calendula, poppies, sunflowers, and zinnias

A gardener who loved fresh cilantro struggled to keep it growing through the heat of summer. Instead of pulling out the plants when they bolted, he let them go to seed. The following spring, cilantro sprouted everywhere, growing exactly when it was ready. He never had to buy cilantro seeds again.

Let Some Plants Go to Seed

To create a self-seeding garden, resist the urge to harvest every last leaf, flower, or vegetable. Allow some plants to complete their full life cycle—blooming, producing seeds, and naturally dropping them into the soil.

For example, if you let a few lettuce plants bolt (grow tall and flower), they'll eventually form seed heads. As the seeds dry, they'll fall into the soil and sprout when the conditions are right. Similarly, a few forgotten cherry tomatoes left on the vine will often drop and sprout new plants in the spring.

One gardener, tired of constantly replanting her greens, allowed a patch of kale to flower in late spring. By fall, tiny kale seedlings were sprouting everywhere. She never had to start kale from seed again.

Minimal Disturbance for Maximum Growth

Once seeds have fallen, avoid over-tilling or heavily mulching the area. Many seeds need light and direct contact with the soil to germinate. Instead, practice light cultivation by gently raking the soil in the fall or early spring to help distribute the seeds without burying them too deeply.

A small-scale farmer noticed that every year, certain areas of his land would be covered in self-seeded mustard greens and dill. The key, he realized, was that those areas were left undisturbed, allowing the seeds to settle naturally and sprout at their own pace.

Watering and Natural Germination

Nature knows best when it comes to timing. Many self-seeded plants germinate with seasonal rains, sprouting when the conditions are just right. While some seedlings may need light watering in dry periods, most will emerge without any extra care.

One urban gardener found tiny tomato plants popping up all over her backyard every spring. She never watered them deliberately—she simply let nature take its course. Those plants often outperformed the ones she carefully started indoors.

Weeding vs. Letting Grow

At first, self-seeding gardens can look a little wild. It takes a trained eye to distinguish between a weed and a valuable seedling. The best approach is to wait and see—if a plant looks familiar, let it grow. Over time, gardeners develop an instinct for recognizing self-seeded vegetables and flowers.

A permaculture enthusiast once let an entire bed of "mystery greens" grow in early spring. Instead of pulling them up, she waited to see what they became. It turned out to be a mix of lettuce, arugula, and mustard from the previous season's crops. She had a free salad garden without lifting a finger.

The Joy of a Self-Sustaining Garden

A self-seeding garden is not only practical and cost-effective—it's a joyful way to garden. There's something magical about seeing plants return year after year, as if the garden itself is taking part in the work. By embracing self-seeding, gardeners can spend less time planting and more time harvesting, while also working in harmony with nature.

UPCYCLED TRELLISES & VERTICAL GARDENING SOLUTIONS

Vertical gardening is one of the most efficient ways to maximize space, improve yields, and create a visually stunning garden. However, store-bought trellises, plant supports, and vertical structures can be expensive. Fortunately, with a little creativity, it's possible to build sturdy, functional, and beautiful trellises from upcycled materials—saving money while reducing waste.

The Beauty of Vertical Gardening

Growing upward instead of outward has numerous benefits. It allows gardeners with limited space to grow more food, improves air circulation (reducing disease), and makes harvesting easier. Vining crops like cucumbers, beans, peas, and even melons thrive when given the right support. Many flowers, too, such as climbing roses and morning glories, flourish when they can climb.

A small-space gardener once turned a bare balcony into a lush oasis by training cucumbers, cherry tomatoes, and pole beans up a series of salvaged wire racks. What started as an experiment became a fully functional, productive vertical garden—without spending a dime on fancy trellises.

Upcycled Trellis Ideas: Turning Scraps into Supports

Instead of buying new garden structures, many everyday materials can be repurposed into trellises. These solutions are often sturdier, more unique, and perfectly suited to the garden's needs.

Old Bed Frames & Headboards

Metal or wooden bed frames, especially those with ornate headboards, make fantastic trellises. Their built-in structure provides strong support for climbing plants like peas and cucumbers. Simply position them against a fence or wall, or anchor them in the ground with stakes.

A gardener once salvaged an antique iron headboard from a neighbor's trash pile and repurposed it into a stunning bean trellis. By the end of summer, it was covered in green vines and bright blossoms, transforming a discarded item into a functional garden feature.

Ladders & Wooden Pallets

Old wooden ladders, especially those with missing rungs, can be repurposed as trellises for climbing flowers and vining vegetables. Pallets, too, offer endless possibilities—they can be stood upright against a wall for peas and beans or laid flat and filled with soil to create a vertical herb garden.

One urban gardener built a "pallet wall" along a sunny side of her apartment courtyard, filling the gaps with pockets of soil and herbs. With no money spent, she had an instant, space-saving vertical garden.

Bicycle Wheels & Wire Fencing

Old bicycle wheels, when stacked and connected with twine or wire, make a perfect circular trellis for vining crops. Likewise, discarded wire fencing, even slightly bent or rusted, can be used to create a sturdy A-frame trellis.

A resourceful farmer once built a DIY bean tunnel using nothing but salvaged fencing and old metal rods. As the beans climbed and intertwined overhead, it created a shady, productive walkway—both practical and beautiful.

Branches & Bamboo Poles

For a rustic, natural look, fallen branches or bamboo poles can be tied together to create teepees, arched trellises, or simple vertical supports. This is an especially useful method for pole beans, tomatoes, and gourds.

A gardener who lived near a wooded area never bought a trellis in her life. Instead, she gathered sturdy fallen branches each spring, tying them into simple supports for peas and beans. Each year, nature provided her with free materials.

Creative Vertical Gardening Solutions

Trellises are just one part of vertical gardening. Other creative ways to grow upwards include:

- **Hanging planters from upcycled containers** – Old buckets, milk jugs, or fabric bags can be turned into hanging baskets for strawberries, herbs, or trailing flowers.
- **Gutter gardens** – Discarded rain gutters mounted on a fence or wall make excellent planters for shallow-rooted crops like lettuce and radishes.
- **Repurposed shelving** – Old bookshelves, spice racks, or wooden crates can be stacked or mounted to create a vertical herb or flower garden.

A retired teacher once turned an old wooden shoe rack into a stunning herb garden by placing small pots in each compartment. With minimal effort, she had a beautiful, functional growing space on her tiny porch.

Sustainable Gardening: Growing Up for Less

Upcycled trellises and vertical gardening solutions prove that resourcefulness and sustainability go hand in hand. By reusing materials, gardeners save money, reduce waste, and create one-of-a-kind structures that serve both function and beauty. Whether it's an old bed frame covered in morning glories or a ladder repurposed for climbing peas, the best gardening solutions often come from looking at discarded items with a fresh perspective.

A thriving vertical garden doesn't have to come with a hefty price tag—it just takes a little ingenuity, a willingness to experiment, and an eye for repurposing the forgotten into something useful.

CHAPTER 6

JUNE: THE PEAK HARVEST—SAVING & PRESERVING

June marks the height of the gardening season, where plants are producing at full speed, and harvest baskets are overflowing. While this abundance is exciting, it can also be overwhelming—especially if more food is ripening than can be eaten fresh. Instead of letting any of this hard-earned produce go to waste, a smart gardener knows that preserving food is key to stretching the harvest and saving money long after the growing season ends.

Fortunately, food preservation doesn't have to be expensive. While canning requires specialized equipment, methods like freezing, drying, and fermenting are low-cost, beginner-friendly ways to store food for months without breaking the budget. These simple techniques allow gardeners to enjoy homegrown flavors deep into winter, reducing grocery bills and making the most of every last vegetable, fruit, and herb.

FREEZING: THE EASIEST AND MOST ACCESSIBLE PRESERVATION METHOD

Freezing is one of the simplest and quickest ways to preserve food. Unlike canning, which requires jars and sterilization, freezing requires only basic supplies—freezer bags, airtight containers, or repurposed glass jars (with enough headspace for expansion). It locks in nutrients and freshness without the need for added preservatives.

Best Crops for Freezing

Many vegetables and fruits freeze beautifully with minimal preparation:

- **Vegetables:** Green beans, peas, corn, bell peppers, spinach, kale, zucchini (grated), and broccoli
- **Fruits:** Berries, peaches, cherries, mangoes, and bananas
- **Herbs:** Basil, parsley, dill, cilantro (best frozen in oil or water)

One thrifty homesteader once shared how she never let a single green bean go to waste. Each day, she would pick just a handful—too few for a full meal. Instead of tossing them aside, she blanched them quickly, packed them into a freezer bag, and kept adding more over time. By season's end, she had several full bags of homegrown beans, ready for soups and stir-fries all winter.

Blanching: The Key to Long-Lasting Frozen Vegetables

Most vegetables benefit from a quick blanching process before freezing. This means briefly boiling or steaming them, then plunging them into ice water to stop the cooking. Blanching helps preserve color, texture, and flavor while reducing spoilage.

A market gardener once learned this lesson the hard way when she skipped blanching her homegrown peas. Within a few months, they had turned mushy and unappetizing in the freezer. After switching to the proper method, she was amazed at how fresh they tasted, even in the middle of winter.

Freezing Tips for Maximum Savings

- **Label everything** – Mark bags or containers with the date and contents to avoid food waste.
- **Use ice cube trays** – Freeze chopped herbs, tomato paste, or even pesto in small portions, then pop them out into a storage bag for easy use.

- **Lay items flat** – Spread out berries, peppers, or shredded zucchini on a baking sheet before bagging to prevent clumping.

Drying: Preserving Food Without Electricity

Drying food is one of the oldest and most budget-friendly preservation methods. Dehydrated foods take up little space, require no refrigeration, and can last for months or even years. A dehydrator is helpful, but an oven, air-drying, or sun-drying also works for many foods.

Best Crops for Drying

- **Fruits:** Apples, pears, bananas, berries, cherries, tomatoes
- **Vegetables:** Mushrooms, peppers, onions, garlic, zucchini, sweet potatoes
- **Herbs:** Oregano, thyme, rosemary, sage, mint, basil

A resourceful gardener once built a simple drying rack from old window screens and set it outside in the summer sun. Within a few days, she had crisp, dried basil and oregano—completely free of cost. She stored them in glass jars and used them for seasoning all winter.

Easy DIY Drying Methods

- **Oven drying:** Set an oven to its lowest temperature (150–170°F), spread thinly sliced food on a baking sheet, and prop the door slightly open for air circulation.
- **Sun drying:** Best for dry, warm climates—place sliced fruits or herbs on a mesh screen and cover with cheesecloth to protect from insects.
- **String drying:** Hang bundles of herbs or hot peppers in a dry, airy space until completely dried.

Fermenting: A No-Cost, Nutrient-Rich Preservation Method

Fermentation is one of the most powerful preservation methods, transforming fresh produce into probiotic-rich, gut-healthy foods. Unlike canning or freezing, fermentation requires no electricity and only basic ingredients—often just salt, water, and time. This process not only extends the shelf life of vegetables but also enhances their nutritional value.

Best Vegetables for Fermenting

- **Cabbage (sauerkraut, kimchi)**
- **Cucumbers (homemade pickles)**
- **Carrots, beets, and radishes**
- **Green beans, garlic, and peppers**

A farmer once shared how his grandmother never let a single cabbage go to waste. Instead of storing heads in a cellar, she shredded them, mixed them with salt, and packed them into a ceramic crock. In a few weeks, she had a tangy, probiotic-rich sauerkraut that kept all winter—without refrigeration.

How to Ferment Vegetables for Free

1. **Chop or shred vegetables** – Cabbage, carrots, radishes, or cucumbers work well.
2. **Massage with salt** – About 1–2% of the vegetable's weight in salt helps draw out water and create a natural brine.
3. **Pack tightly into a jar** – Press vegetables down so they are fully submerged in their own juices (add extra brine if needed).
4. **Weigh them down** – Use a clean rock or a small jar to keep everything submerged.

5. **Let it ferment** – Store at room temperature for a few days to weeks, tasting until it reaches the desired tanginess.

Within a few weeks, what started as simple cabbage becomes flavorful sauerkraut, and plain cucumbers transform into probiotic-rich pickles—without a single dollar spent on expensive preservation methods.

Preserving the Harvest for Year-Round Savings

By using freezing, drying, and fermenting, gardeners can extend the bounty of summer far beyond the growing season. These methods require little to no special equipment and save money on store-bought foods while reducing waste. A well-stocked freezer, pantry, or fermentation crock means that even in the depths of winter, the flavors of a thriving summer garden can still be enjoyed—one frozen berry, dried tomato, or tangy pickle at a time.

Smart food preservation isn't just about saving money—it's about creating a self-sufficient, waste-free lifestyle where every harvest is used to its fullest potential. With a bit of planning and creativity, any gardener can enjoy the taste of homegrown food all year long, for next to nothing.

BUILDING A DIY SOLAR DEHYDRATOR: A ZERO-COST WAY TO PRESERVE FOOD

Dehydrating food is one of the oldest and most effective ways to preserve harvests, allowing fruits, vegetables, and herbs to be stored for months without refrigeration. While electric dehydrators can be expensive and energy-consuming, a DIY solar dehydrator offers a completely free, off-grid way to dry food using nothing but the sun's energy.

By building a simple solar dehydrator with salvaged or low-cost materials, gardeners can create a sustainable food preservation system that lasts for years. Whether drying tomatoes, herbs, apples, or mushrooms, this method ensures that no garden abundance ever goes to waste.

Why Build a Solar Dehydrator?

- **No electricity required** – Uses only the sun, making it perfect for off-grid or eco-conscious living.
- **Preserves food for free** – Eliminates the cost of running an electric dehydrator or oven.
- **Sustainable and long-lasting** – A well-built solar dehydrator can be used year after year.
- **More efficient than air-drying** – Speeds up the drying process by trapping heat and allowing proper airflow.

A resourceful homesteader once shared how he turned an old wooden box and scrap window glass into a highly efficient solar dehydrator. Over the years, he dried everything from apples to hot peppers, storing hundreds of pounds of produce for free.

Solar Dehydrator

How to Build a DIY Solar Dehydrator

Materials Needed (Most Can Be Salvaged)

- **A wooden box or frame** (old dresser drawers, scrap wood, or plywood)
- **A piece of clear glass or plastic** (old window panes or acrylic sheets)
- **Wire mesh or food-safe screens** (recycled window screens or drying racks)
- **Ventilation holes** (drilled into the box for airflow)
- **Black paint or foil** (to absorb heat)
- **Bricks or wooden blocks** (to elevate the dehydrator for airflow)

A gardener who lived in a rural area once built his solar dehydrator entirely from salvaged materials. By repurposing an old picture frame for the glass and using a discarded wooden crate, he assembled a fully functional drying system at no cost.

Step-by-Step Guide to Building a Solar Dehydrator

1. Build or Repurpose a Box for the Drying Chamber

Start with a sturdy wooden box—this will act as the main drying chamber. An old dresser drawer, wooden crate, or plywood nailed together works well. Ensure it has enough depth to hold multiple drying racks.

2. Create Proper Airflow

Drill small ventilation holes at the bottom and top of the box. Warm air rises, so these vents will allow fresh air to circulate, preventing mold and ensuring even drying.

3. Add a Transparent Cover

Attach a piece of clear glass or acrylic to the top of the box. This creates a greenhouse effect, trapping heat inside while allowing sunlight to penetrate.

4. Increase Heat Absorption

Paint the inside of the box black or line it with aluminum foil to absorb and distribute heat more efficiently. This step significantly speeds up the drying process.

5. Install Drying Racks

Use wire mesh, food-safe screens, or wooden slats to create drying racks. These should be stacked inside the box, allowing air to circulate around the food. Herbs and small fruits can be placed directly on the screens, while larger items like sliced apples or tomatoes should be evenly spaced.

6. Elevate the Dehydrator

Place the dehydrator on bricks or wooden blocks to improve airflow underneath. Position it at an angle facing the sun for maximum heat absorption.

Using Your Solar Dehydrator

Once the dehydrator is built, it's time to start drying!

Best Foods for Solar Drying

- **Fruits:** Apples, peaches, bananas, figs, grapes (for raisins)
- **Vegetables:** Tomatoes, bell peppers, mushrooms, zucchini, onions
- **Herbs:** Basil, oregano, mint, thyme, rosemary

How to Dry Food Efficiently

1. **Slice food thinly** – Thinner pieces dry faster and more evenly.
2. **Arrange in a single layer** – Avoid overlapping to ensure proper airflow.
3. **Place in full sun** – Choose a spot with at least 6–8 hours of direct sunlight.
4. **Check regularly** – Depending on humidity and temperature, drying may take 1–3 days.
5. **Store properly** – Once completely dry, store in airtight jars or vacuum-sealed bags.

A seasoned gardener once experimented with drying tomatoes in his DIY solar dehydrator. At first, he left them too thick, and they took days to dry. After slicing them thinner and positioning the dehydrator to catch maximum sun, he was able to dry whole batches in just two days—without spending a single dollar on electricity.

Sustainable Food Preservation for a Lifetime

A DIY solar dehydrator is one of the best investments a frugal gardener can make. With a bit of effort and resourcefulness, anyone can build a functional, cost-free drying system that lasts for years. It not only reduces food waste but also provides a steady supply of dried fruits, vegetables, and herbs—ensuring that no part of the garden's abundance goes to waste.

MAKING YOUR OWN ORGANIC FERTILIZERS FROM GARDEN WASTE

Fertilizing a garden doesn't have to mean spending money on commercial products. The healthiest, most cost-effective way to feed plants is by making organic fertilizers from what's already available—garden waste, kitchen scraps, and natural materials. These homemade fertilizers not only nourish plants but also improve soil health, reduce waste, and create a closed-loop system where nothing goes unused.

For generations, gardeners have relied on compost, manure, and natural amendments to keep their soil fertile. One experienced grower once shared how he transformed a struggling vegetable patch simply by using composted leaves and homemade compost tea. By working with nature instead of against it, he built a thriving, self-sustaining garden—without spending a dime on store-bought fertilizers.

The Power of Garden Waste as Fertilizer

Every year, tons of organic waste end up in landfills when they could be feeding gardens instead. Leaves, grass clippings, kitchen scraps, weeds, and even spent crops are rich in nutrients that plants need to grow. The key to making effective organic fertilizers is understanding how to break down these materials and release their nutrients back into the soil.

Three Main Nutrients Plants Need

- **Nitrogen (N)** – Promotes leafy growth (found in grass clippings, coffee grounds, manure).
- **Phosphorus (P)** – Supports root development (found in banana peels, bone meal, eggshells).
- **Potassium (K)** – Strengthens plants and improves resistance to disease (found in wood ash, composted fruit scraps, seaweed).

By using the right combination of these elements, a gardener can create balanced, homemade fertilizers that rival anything found in stores.

How to Make Organic Fertilizers from Garden Waste

1. Compost: The Ultimate All-Purpose Fertilizer

Compost is often called "black gold" because it enriches the soil with a full spectrum of nutrients while improving texture, aeration, and moisture retention. The best part? It's made entirely from food scraps, plant debris, and garden waste.

How to Make Compost for Maximum Fertility

1. **Layer greens and browns** – Combine nitrogen-rich materials (grass clippings, fruit peels) with carbon-rich materials (dried leaves, cardboard).
2. **Turn regularly** – Aerating the pile helps it break down faster and prevents odors.
3. **Keep it moist** – Like a damp sponge, not too wet or too dry.

4. **Wait and harvest** – In a few months, the waste transforms into rich, dark compost that can be mixed into garden beds or used as mulch.

A frugal gardener once discovered that his neglected pile of autumn leaves had turned into dark, crumbly compost by spring. Instead of buying expensive soil amendments, he spread the compost over his garden beds, and his vegetables thrived like never before.

2. Compost Tea: Liquid Gold for Plants

Compost tea is an easy, free way to create a fast-acting liquid fertilizer that boosts plant health. It extracts nutrients and beneficial microbes from compost into a form that plants can absorb quickly.

How to Make Compost Tea

1. Fill a bucket with water (preferably rainwater).
2. Add a shovel of finished compost or aged manure.
3. Stir daily and let steep for 3–5 days.
4. Strain and use the liquid to water plants or as a foliar spray.

This simple fertilizer is often called "instant plant food" because it delivers nutrients directly to roots and leaves. A market gardener once credited compost tea for reviving his struggling tomato plants mid-season, giving them a boost without any synthetic fertilizers.

3. Grass Clipping Fertilizer: A Free Source of Nitrogen

Fresh grass clippings are an excellent nitrogen source, ideal for boosting leafy vegetables and young plants. Instead of bagging and discarding lawn clippings, they can be used directly in the garden.

How to Use Grass Clippings as Fertilizer

- **Mulch:** Spread a thin layer around plants to slowly release nitrogen.
- **Compost addition:** Balance with dry materials like leaves.
- **Fermented grass tea:** Soak clippings in water for a few days to make a nutrient-rich liquid fertilizer.

A resourceful homesteader once shared how she never let a single blade of grass go to waste. By spreading clippings under her tomato plants, she not only fertilized them but also suppressed weeds and retained moisture—all for free.

4. Banana Peel Fertilizer: A Natural Boost for Flowers and Fruits

Banana peels are rich in potassium and phosphorus, essential for flower and fruit development. Instead of tossing them in the trash, they can be turned into a simple homemade fertilizer.

Ways to Use Banana Peels as Fertilizer

- **Bury them** – Place chopped peels directly in the soil near plants.
- **Banana tea** – Soak peels in water for a few days and use the liquid to water plants.
- **Dry and grind** – Make potassium-rich powder to sprinkle around flowers and vegetables.

A flower grower once experimented with banana peels around her roses. Within weeks, she noticed stronger stems and more vibrant blooms, proving that expensive fertilizers aren't necessary when nature provides its own solutions.

5. Eggshell Fertilizer: Free Calcium for Stronger Plants

Eggshells are one of the best natural sources of calcium, which helps prevent blossom-end rot in tomatoes, peppers, and squash. Instead of throwing them away, they can be ground into a free soil amendment.

How to Use Eggshells in the Garden

- **Crush and sprinkle** – Scatter crushed shells around plants to add calcium.
- **Eggshell tea** – Soak in water for a few days and use as a liquid fertilizer.
- **Mix into compost** – Slowly releases nutrients as it breaks down.

One backyard gardener swore by eggshell tea for preventing tomato rot. After suffering losses one year, he started soaking shells and pouring the water at the base of his plants. That season, every single tomato ripened perfectly.

6. Wood Ash: A Free Source of Potassium and pH Balance

For those with a fireplace or firepit, wood ash can be a valuable, no-cost fertilizer. It's rich in potassium and helps raise soil pH, making it useful for acidic soils.

How to Use Wood Ash Wisely

- **Sprinkle lightly around plants** – Especially beneficial for fruiting crops.
- **Mix into compost** – Helps balance acidity.
- **Make ash tea** – Steep in water for a liquid potassium boost.

One thrifty gardener discovered that a small handful of wood ash around his squash plants made them grow more vigorously. Over time, he realized he had a completely free fertilizer source sitting in his own backyard.

THE CHEAPEST WAY TO STAKE, CAGE, AND SUPPORT PLANTS

Supporting plants properly is essential for healthier growth, higher yields, and easier harvesting. However, many gardeners spend a small fortune on commercial trellises, cages, and stakes when plenty of free or low-cost alternatives exist. By using salvaged materials, natural resources, and a bit of creativity, gardeners can provide strong, long-lasting support systems without breaking the bank.

A seasoned homesteader once turned his overgrown backyard into a thriving vegetable garden without spending a dime on plant supports. He repurposed old furniture, trimmed branches, and even used discarded fencing to stake tomatoes, beans, and cucumbers. Not only did he save money, but his plants thrived in their upcycled structures, proving that effective gardening doesn't have to come with a high price tag.

Why Proper Plant Support Matters

Many plants—especially vining and heavy-fruiting crops—need support to:

- **Prevent breakage** – Helps plants withstand wind, rain, and their own weight.
- **Reduce disease** – Keeps foliage off the ground, preventing rot and fungal infections.
- **Improve yields** – Ensures better air circulation, sunlight exposure, and easier pollination.

- **Save space** – Allows vertical growth, making the most of small gardens.

A gardener who once struggled with disease-prone tomatoes learned that a simple trellis system kept his plants healthier and doubled his harvest. Instead of dealing with rotting fruit and tangled vines, he enjoyed clean, easy-to-pick produce all season long.

Budget-Friendly Ways to Stake, Cage, and Support Plants

1. Staking with Free or Salvaged Materials

Many plants, including tomatoes, peppers, and eggplants, benefit from individual stakes. Instead of buying expensive bamboo or metal rods, consider:

- **Tree branches** – Trimmed limbs from pruning fruit trees or shrubs make sturdy, natural stakes.
- **Scrap lumber** – Leftover wooden planks, broom handles, or cut-up pallets work well.
- **Metal pipes or rebar** – Salvaged from construction sites or old fencing.
- **Bamboo from a neighbor's yard** – Many gardeners will gladly share bamboo if asked.

To stake plants effectively, push the support firmly into the ground near the plant and secure it with soft ties like strips of old T-shirts or natural twine.

A frugal gardener once collected straight branches after a storm, stripping off the bark and using them as tomato stakes for years. His simple, no-cost solution outperformed store-bought stakes, which often broke under pressure.

2. DIY Plant Cages for Pennies

Plant cages provide all-around support, especially for bushy crops like tomatoes and peppers. Instead of buying costly metal cages, try:

- **Reusing old fencing** – Cut sections of wire fencing and shape them into cylinders.
- **Concrete reinforcement wire** – Found at hardware stores or scrap yards, this material lasts for years.
- **Broken laundry baskets** – The frames make excellent DIY plant cages.
- **Upcycled bicycle rims** – Stacked and tied together, they create strong, circular cages.

To make a free tomato cage, cut a length of old wire fencing, form it into a tube, and secure the ends together. Push the cage into the soil around the plant, and it will provide sturdy, long-term support.

A rural gardener once used discarded fencing from a neighbor's yard to build dozens of tomato cages. They lasted over a decade, saving her hundreds of dollars while keeping her plants upright and healthy.

3. Free or Cheap Trellises for Climbing Plants

Vining crops like peas, beans, cucumbers, and squash thrive when grown vertically. Trellises not only save space but also make harvesting easier. Instead of store-bought versions, try:

- **Branches and saplings** – Lash together to form a rustic, natural trellis.
- **Old ladders** – Lean against a fence for a built-in climbing frame.
- **Discarded bed frames** – The metal bars make sturdy, long-lasting supports.

- **Wooden pallets** – Stood upright, they provide a ready-made trellis.
- **Wire mesh or old screen doors** – Perfect for climbing beans or gourds.

For a nearly free cucumber trellis, drive two stakes into the ground and string salvaged twine or wire between them. The vines will naturally cling and climb, keeping the fruit off the ground.

A market grower once used an old metal bed frame as a cucumber trellis. By the end of the season, it was covered in vines, and he harvested over 50 pounds of cucumbers—all from a structure that had cost him nothing.

4. Repurposed Household Items for Plant Support

Many everyday household objects can be turned into excellent plant supports, including:

- **Old pantyhose or T-shirts** – Cut into strips for soft, flexible plant ties.
- **Wire coat hangers** – Bent into shape for individual plant stakes or hoops.
- **Broken umbrellas** – The metal ribs make great lightweight trellises.
- **Tomato cages flipped upside-down** – Used as supports for vining squash or flowers.

A resourceful gardener once found an old crib frame at a yard sale and repurposed the metal bars into an arched bean trellis. It became the highlight of his garden, producing abundant pole beans while costing almost nothing.

FREE PEST CONTROL STRATEGIES: DIY SPRAYS, BENEFICIAL INSECTS, AND TRAP CROPS

Keeping pests at bay is one of the biggest challenges in gardening, and many people assume they need expensive pesticides to protect their crops. However, some of the most effective pest control methods are completely free and work in harmony with nature rather than against it. From homemade sprays to attracting beneficial insects, gardeners can reduce or eliminate pests without spending a dime.

One experienced gardener once struggled with an aphid infestation that threatened her entire vegetable garden. Instead of resorting to costly chemical sprays, she introduced ladybugs and used a simple homemade garlic spray. Within weeks, the aphid population collapsed, and her plants thrived. The lesson was clear: nature provides solutions when we work with it instead of fighting against it.

1. DIY Pest Sprays: Simple, Safe, and Effective

Homemade sprays use everyday kitchen ingredients to deter pests without harming plants, pollinators, or soil health. Unlike chemical pesticides, they break down naturally, leaving no toxic residue behind.

Garlic and Chili Spray (All-Purpose Insect Repellent)

This potent mixture repels aphids, caterpillars, and beetles.

How to Make It:

1. Blend 1 garlic bulb and 1 hot pepper with 2 cups of water.
2. Let it sit overnight, then strain into a spray bottle.
3. Add a few drops of dish soap to help it stick to leaves.
4. Spray on plants every few days, especially after rain.

Soap Spray (Soft-Bodied Insect Killer)

Kills aphids, spider mites, and whiteflies by suffocating them.

How to Make It:

1. Mix 1 teaspoon of mild dish soap with 1 quart of water.
2. Spray directly onto infested plants, making sure to coat the undersides of leaves.
3. Repeat every few days until pests disappear.

Neem Oil Spray (Natural Fungicide & Insect Repellent)

Neem oil, extracted from neem tree seeds, disrupts the life cycle of many garden pests.

How to Make It:

1. Mix 1 teaspoon of neem oil with 1 quart of water.
2. Add a few drops of dish soap and shake well.
3. Spray in the early morning or late evening to avoid harming beneficial insects.

A resourceful farmer once replaced his entire pesticide routine with DIY sprays. Not only did he save money, but his soil health improved, and his garden became a haven for pollinators.

2. Attracting Beneficial Insects: Nature's Pest Control

Not all insects are enemies—some are natural predators of common garden pests. By creating a habitat that attracts beneficial bugs, gardeners can maintain a self-sustaining, low-cost pest control system.

Top Beneficial Insects and How to Attract Them

- **Ladybugs** – Devour aphids, mites, and whiteflies. (*Plant dill, fennel, and marigolds to invite them in.*)
- **Lacewings** – Their larvae eat thrips, aphids, and mealybugs. (*Grow coriander, cosmos, and alyssum.*)
- **Praying Mantises** – Eat almost any garden pest. (*Leave tall grass and shrubs as shelter.*)
- **Hoverflies** – Their larvae feed on aphids. (*Plant yarrow, sunflowers, and chamomile.*)

One gardener who struggled with whiteflies planted alyssum and dill around his garden. Within a few weeks, hoverflies moved in and wiped out the infestation—proving that nature often solves its own problems when given the chance.

3. Trap Crops: Sacrificing a Few Plants to Save Many

Trap cropping is an old gardening technique where specific plants attract pests away from main crops. These "sacrificial" plants take the damage while the primary harvest remains untouched.

Best Trap Crops for Common Pests

- **Nasturtiums** – Attract aphids away from vegetables.
- **Radishes** – Lure flea beetles away from leafy greens.
- **Mustard greens** – Sacrifice to cabbage worms and harlequin bugs.
- **Sunflowers** – Draw stink bugs away from tomatoes.

A homesteader once found his squash plants riddled with cucumber beetles. The following year, he planted a patch of blue hubbard squash far from his main crops. The pests flocked to the hubbard and left his zucchini untouched, proving that sometimes the best way to win against pests is by giving them something else to eat.

4. Companion Planting for Pest Control

Certain plant combinations naturally deter pests, reducing the need for sprays.

Effective Companion Plant Pairings

- **Tomatoes + Basil** – Repels hornworms and enhances tomato flavor.
- **Carrots + Onions** – Onions deter carrot flies, and carrots deter onion flies.
- **Cabbage + Thyme** – Thyme repels cabbage worms.
- **Beans + Marigolds** – Marigolds deter nematodes and beetles.

An urban gardener once had a terrible problem with cabbage worms. Instead of using chemicals, she planted thyme throughout her cabbage patch. The worms disappeared, and her cabbages flourished—proving that sometimes the best pest control is just planting the right combinations.

5. Natural Barriers and Physical Controls

Row Covers

A lightweight fabric draped over plants keeps out pests like cabbage moths and squash bugs while allowing sunlight and rain through. Old sheer curtains or tulle fabric work just as well as expensive garden covers.

Handpicking Pests

Some pests, like hornworms and Japanese beetles, are best controlled by handpicking. Drop them into a bucket of soapy water to dispose of them quickly.

Diatomaceous Earth (DE)

This natural powder, made from fossilized algae, dehydrates and kills soft-bodied insects like slugs and beetles. Sprinkle lightly around plants to create a protective barrier.

A small-scale organic farmer once relied entirely on row covers and diatomaceous earth to keep pests off his greens. While neighbors sprayed chemicals, he harvested clean, chemical-free produce with almost no pest damage.

CHAPTER 7

JULY: KEEPING THE GARDEN THRIVING WITHOUT EXTRA COSTS

July brings the heat, and with it, the challenge of keeping plants hydrated without skyrocketing water bills. Many gardeners assume that more water equals better growth, but the truth is, excessive watering can lead to weak root systems, fungal diseases, and wasted resources. The key is not just using less water but using it wisely.

A seasoned homesteader once faced a summer drought that left nearby gardens struggling. While others rushed to install expensive irrigation systems, he relied on traditional water-saving techniques: buried clay pots, deep mulch, and greywater reuse. His garden thrived despite the heat, proving that the right strategies make all the difference—without costing a fortune.

1. Olla Pots: Ancient Irrigation for the Modern Gardener

One of the most efficient ways to water plants with minimal waste is using **olla pots**—an ancient method still widely used in arid regions.

How It Works:

An unglazed clay pot is buried near plants with only the top exposed. When filled with water, moisture slowly seeps through the porous walls, delivering water directly to the roots as needed.

How to Make a DIY Olla:

- Use an unglazed terracotta pot with a drainage hole.
- Seal the hole with a cork or waterproof sealant.

- Bury the pot up to its rim near thirsty plants.
- Fill it with water, and let plants draw moisture as needed.

Olla pots

A frugal gardener once placed a series of ollas in her raised beds, filling them just once a week. Despite record-high temperatures, her vegetables remained lush and healthy with almost no extra effort.

2. Deep Mulching: Nature's Best Moisture Lock

Mulch is one of the simplest and most cost-effective ways to retain moisture, regulate soil temperature, and suppress weeds. A **thick layer of organic mulch** (4–6 inches) can cut water use by up to 50%.

Best Free Mulch Options:

- **Grass clippings** – Retain moisture and add nitrogen to the soil.
- **Shredded leaves** – Decompose slowly, improving soil structure.

- **Wood chips** – Excellent for pathways and fruit trees.
- **Straw or hay** – Great for vegetable gardens, but ensure it's seed-free.

How to Apply Mulch for Maximum Water Savings:

1. Water the soil deeply before adding mulch.
2. Apply a **4–6 inch layer** around plants, keeping it a few inches away from stems.
3. Replenish as needed, especially during hot months.

One market gardener, known for growing tomatoes without irrigation, swore by deep mulching. He covered his entire garden with thick layers of straw and grass clippings, reducing watering to just once every two weeks—even during peak summer.

3. Greywater Use: Reusing Water Safely

Greywater—gently used household water from sinks, showers, and laundry—can be a **free** and **sustainable** irrigation source. Instead of letting water go down the drain, it can be repurposed for deep-rooted plants, trees, and shrubs.

Simple Ways to Collect Greywater:

- **Bucket in the shower** – Catch excess water while waiting for it to warm up.
- **Sink water collection** – Use a dishpan to gather rinse water for outdoor use.
- **Laundry-to-Landscape system** – Divert washing machine water (without harmful detergents) to fruit trees.

Where to Use Greywater Safely:

✔ Fruit trees
✔ Ornamental plants
✔ Shrubs and hedges

🚫 Avoid using greywater on leafy greens, root crops, or anything eaten raw.

A resourceful gardener once saved hundreds of gallons of water each month by routing his laundry water to a fruit tree orchard. His trees thrived, and his water bill dropped significantly—all without buying a costly irrigation system.

THE BEST HOMEMADE PLANT FOODS: BANANA PEEL TEA, NETTLE FERTILIZER, AND MORE

Healthy soil is the foundation of a thriving garden, but store-bought fertilizers can be expensive and often contain unnecessary additives. The good news? Some of the best plant foods come from everyday kitchen and garden scraps. By making homemade fertilizers, gardeners can **nourish their plants for free** while reducing waste.

A resourceful gardener once turned her entire garden into a lush, productive space using nothing but homemade fertilizers. With compost tea, banana peels, and nettle-infused water, her plants flourished—proof that nature provides everything needed for success.

1. Banana Peel Tea: A Potassium Boost for Flowering Plants

Banana peels are rich in **potassium, phosphorus, and calcium**—nutrients essential for fruiting and flowering plants like tomatoes, peppers, and roses. Instead of tossing them, turn them into a nutrient-rich liquid fertilizer.

How to Make Banana Peel Tea:

1. Chop up **3-4 banana peels** and place them in a jar.
2. Fill the jar with water and let it sit for **24-48 hours**.
3. Strain and pour the liquid at the base of plants.

This gentle, organic feed encourages stronger stems, more blooms, and better fruit production without any added cost.

2. Nettle Fertilizer: A High-Nitrogen Powerhouse

Stinging nettle is often considered a weed, but it's one of the best natural fertilizers available. Nettles are high in nitrogen, iron, and magnesium, making them perfect for leafy greens and fast-growing plants.

How to Make Nettle Fertilizer:

1. Gather **fresh nettle leaves** (wear gloves!).
2. Fill a bucket with leaves and add water, submerging them.
3. Let the mixture steep for **1-2 weeks**, stirring occasionally.
4. Strain and dilute the liquid **1:10 with water** before using.

This powerful tea stimulates lush growth and deep green foliage—without the cost of commercial fertilizers.

3. Eggshell Tea: Calcium for Stronger Plants

Eggshells contain **calcium**, which prevents blossom end rot in tomatoes, peppers, and squash.

How to Make Eggshell Tea:

1. Crush **6–8 eggshells** and place them in a pot.
2. Add water and simmer for **30 minutes**.
3. Let it cool, strain, and use the water to feed plants.

This simple method strengthens plant cell walls and improves overall growth.

4. Compost Tea: A Balanced All-Purpose Fertilizer

Compost tea is a liquid extract of compost, packed with beneficial microbes and nutrients.

How to Make Compost Tea:

1. Fill a **5-gallon bucket** one-third full with finished compost.
2. Add water, stir, and let it sit for **24–48 hours**.
3. Strain and use the liquid to water plants.

This tea boosts soil health, improves plant resilience, and provides a steady nutrient supply.

By using homemade fertilizers, gardeners can **reduce waste, save money, and build healthier soil naturally**—a true win-win for both plants and the planet.

HOW TO AVOID COSTLY SUMMER GARDEN MISTAKES (Overwatering, Poor Pruning, and More)

Summer is the peak of the gardening season, but it's also a time when small mistakes can lead to plant stress, poor yields, and wasted resources. Many gardeners unknowingly overwater, prune incorrectly, or neglect key maintenance—leading to preventable problems.

An experienced gardener once watched neighbors struggle with yellowing leaves, stunted plants, and pest infestations. The cause? Overwatering, haphazard pruning, and neglecting soil health. By following a few simple principles, he kept his own garden thriving while others struggled.

1. Overwatering: The #1 Cause of Plant Stress

Many gardeners assume more water equals healthier plants, but overwatering **drowns roots, encourages disease, and attracts pests**.

Signs of Overwatering:

- Yellowing leaves that feel soft
- Wilting despite wet soil
- Mold or fungus on the surface

How to Water Correctly in Summer:

✔ Water deeply **once** or twice a week instead of daily.
✔ Water early in the morning to prevent evaporation.
✔ Use drip irrigation, ollas, or deep mulching to retain moisture.

A market grower once cut his water use in half by switching from overhead sprinklers to deep mulching. His plants thrived, his water bill dropped, and he avoided summer fungal outbreaks.

2. Poor Pruning: Cutting at the Wrong Time

Pruning is essential for airflow, fruit production, and disease prevention, but **cutting at the wrong time or in the wrong place can harm plants**.

Common Pruning Mistakes to Avoid:

🚫 Pruning **tomatoes too aggressively** (removing too many leaves exposes fruits to sunscald).
🚫 Cutting **fruit trees in mid-summer** (this weakens them before winter).
🚫 Trimming **woody herbs too late** (this can prevent regrowth).

How to Prune Correctly:

✔ **Pinch tomato suckers** early instead of removing whole branches later.
✔ **Harvest herbs frequently** to encourage bushy growth.
✔ **Thin fruit trees in early summer** to improve airflow and fruit size.

A small orchard owner once lost an entire season's harvest by pruning his fruit trees in July. The lesson? **Timing is everything when it comes to pruning.**

3. Letting Weeds Go to Seed

Weeds steal nutrients, water, and sunlight from crops. **One weed left to flower can produce thousands of seeds**, leading to bigger problems next season.

Preventing a Weed Explosion:

✔ **Remove weeds before they flower**—even if you don't have time to pull the roots.
✔ **Use mulch** to block weed growth.
✔ **Plant cover crops** in empty spaces to crowd out weeds.

An urban gardener once spent years battling weeds until she switched to **thick mulch and no-till methods**. Within one season, her weeding time dropped by 80%.

4. Ignoring Soil Health in the Heat

Hot weather drains nutrients from the soil, and plants growing at full speed need steady feeding.

Summer Soil Care Tips:

✔ Top-dress with compost every few weeks.
✔ Use homemade fertilizers like banana peel tea or compost tea.
✔ Rotate crops to avoid depleting soil nutrients.

One homesteader noticed his cucumbers failing mid-season every year. The fix? A simple layer of compost and a mulch refresh in July kept them producing through August.

5. Forgetting to Protect Against Summer Pests

Heat brings an explosion of pests, from aphids to squash bugs. Many gardeners don't notice infestations until they're out of control.

Early Pest Prevention:

✔ Check leaves daily for eggs and larvae.
✔ Use trap crops (like nasturtiums for aphids).
✔ Release beneficial insects (ladybugs, lacewings).

A community gardener once lost her entire zucchini patch to squash bugs—until she started using floating row covers and companion planting with radishes. The next year, she harvested more than ever.

PRUNING FOR PRODUCTIVITY: GETTING MORE FROM EVERY PLANT

Pruning is one of the most powerful yet overlooked tools for increasing yields. Done correctly, it channels a plant's energy into fruit production rather than excess foliage, leading to larger harvests, healthier plants, and better air circulation. Yet, many gardeners either over-prune, weakening plants, or fail to prune at all, allowing disease and low yields to take hold.

A seasoned gardener once transformed a struggling tomato patch by simply pruning wisely. Before pruning, his plants were sprawling, tangled, and producing tiny fruits. After carefully removing excess growth, he saw an explosion of larger, healthier tomatoes—without using any additional fertilizer or water.

1. Why Pruning Boosts Productivity

Plants have limited energy. Left unpruned, they waste resources growing unnecessary leaves and stems instead of **putting energy into flowers and fruit**. Strategic pruning ensures plants:

- ✔ Produce larger, healthier fruits
- ✔ Have better air circulation (preventing disease)
- ✔ Use nutrients more efficiently

For example, pruning indeterminate tomatoes allows the plant to focus on ripening fruit rather than wasting energy on excessive leaves. Similarly, trimming pepper plants encourages sturdier stems and more branching, leading to a bigger yield.

2. The Right Way to Prune Common Crops

Tomatoes (Indeterminate Varieties Only)

- Remove suckers (the small shoots that grow in the leaf axils).
- Keep no more than 2–3 main stems for best production.
- Never remove more than ⅓ **of the plant at once** to avoid stress.

Peppers

- Prune early in the season to encourage strong branching.
- Remove low-hanging leaves touching the soil to prevent disease.
- If plants become top-heavy, pinch back tips to **strengthen the stems**.

Squash & Cucumbers

- Remove lower leaves to improve airflow and reduce powdery mildew risk.
- Train vines up a trellis to maximize space and prevent rot.

Herbs (Basil, Mint, Oregano, etc.)

- Pinch back frequently to prevent bolting and encourage bushier growth.
- Always cut above a set of leaves to promote branching.

A market grower once doubled his basil yield simply by pruning correctly—harvesting more from **fewer plants** while extending the growing season.

3. Pruning to Extend the Harvest

Strategic pruning can keep plants producing longer. A neglected tomato plant may slow down in late summer, while a well-pruned one continues yielding into fall.

✔ For **tomatoes**, remove older leaves and excess suckers to push energy into ripening fruit.

✔ For **lettuce and leafy greens**, trim outer leaves rather than harvesting the whole plant.

✔ For **herbs**, cut back flower buds to prevent the plant from going to seed too soon.

A homesteader once saved his entire pepper harvest by pruning off excess branches during a heatwave. While other gardens wilted, his plants focused on **producing fruit instead of unnecessary foliage**, keeping yields high despite the stress.

MAKING THE MOST OF SECOND-SEASON PLANTING: FALL CROPS FOR CHEAP

Many gardeners make the mistake of treating summer as the end of the growing season, leaving valuable garden space empty. But a second-season garden—also known as fall planting—can extend the harvest for months with minimal effort and cost.

A gardener once discovered the power of fall planting after watching his summer garden wither in the heat. Instead of letting his beds sit empty, he re-planted with **cold-tolerant crops** like spinach, carrots, and kale. The result? Fresh vegetables long after his neighbors had packed up their gardens for the year.

1. Why Fall Gardening Saves Money

✔ Cooler temperatures = less water needed
✔ Fewer pests = healthier plants with little intervention
✔ Leftover summer compost & mulch feed new crops
✔ Seeds are often cheaper in late summer

With simple planning, a garden can **keep producing into late fall and even winter**, reducing grocery bills while maximizing every inch of space.

2. The Best Second-Season Crops for Maximum Yield

Fall gardening isn't just about planting **cold-hardy crops**—it's also about **choosing fast-growing varieties that mature before frost.**

Leafy Greens (Fast & Cold-Hardy)

- Spinach
- Kale
- Swiss chard
- Lettuce
- Arugula

Most leafy greens thrive in cooler weather, with kale even improving in flavor after a light frost.

Root Crops (Store Well & Grow Late)

- Carrots
- Beets
- Radishes
- Turnips
- Garlic (for a spring harvest)

Carrots and beets can **stay in the ground all winter** under mulch, ready for harvest when needed.

Legumes (Soil Builders & Fast Growers)

- Snow peas
- Shelling peas
- Bush beans (if planted early enough)

Peas planted in late summer **fix nitrogen** in the soil, improving fertility for the next season.

3. How to Transition from Summer to Fall Crops

Many gardeners hesitate to plant a second season, fearing they'll need extra space or new garden beds. But in reality, fall crops can go right into spaces left by summer plants—no extra work needed.

Step-by-Step Fall Planting Guide:

1. **Clear spent summer plants** (remove tomatoes, peppers, or cucumbers as they finish producing).
2. **Refresh the soil** with compost to replenish nutrients.
3. **Direct sow seeds** for root crops and leafy greens.
4. **Water well and mulch** to retain moisture.

One frugal gardener once stretched her harvest into December simply by replanting fast-growing greens in September. With no extra cost, she enjoyed fresh salads while others relied on store-bought produce.

4. Protecting Fall Crops for a Longer Harvest

Even in colder climates, **simple protection** can extend the growing season:

✔ **Row covers or fleece blankets** trap warmth during chilly nights.
✔ **Cold frames (made from old windows)** provide a greenhouse effect.
✔ **Mulching with straw or leaves** insulates root crops for winter harvest.

One small-scale farmer once used a row of salvaged windows to build a makeshift cold frame, allowing him to harvest greens well into January—without spending a dime.

A Year-Round Garden Without Extra Cost

By replanting after summer, gardeners double their harvest without buying more land, water, or expensive supplies. The key is choosing the right crops, using available space wisely, and taking advantage of natural seasonal shifts.

A truly money-saving garden doesn't stop when summer ends—it keeps feeding its gardener deep into fall and beyond, proving that with the right strategies, fresh food can be enjoyed all year long for almost no extra cost.

AUGUST: SEED SAVING & PERENNIAL PROPAGATION

August marks a pivotal moment in the frugal gardener's year—the height of the harvest, but also a time to think ahead. As summer crops reach maturity, they offer an often-overlooked treasure: seeds for next year's garden. Meanwhile, perennials can be propagated to expand a garden without spending a dime.

Many experienced gardeners view August not just as a time to reap what they've sown, but as an opportunity to secure future harvests for free. A small backyard gardener once transformed his plot into a thriving, self-sustaining oasis by saving seeds and propagating plants year after year. With each season, his garden grew richer, more resilient, and less expensive to maintain.

This chapter explores how to save seeds from common vegetables and herbs while also multiplying perennials, ensuring that a garden keeps producing season after season without breaking the budget.

SAVING SEEDS FROM COMMON VEGETABLES AND HERBS

Seed saving is one of the most powerful money-saving skills a gardener can develop. Instead of buying packets every spring, a well-managed garden can provide nearly all the seeds needed for the following year. Over time, these saved seeds adapt to local conditions, becoming hardier and more productive.

How to Choose the Best Seeds to Save

Not all seeds are worth saving. The best choices come from **open-pollinated (heirloom) plants**, which produce offspring true to the parent plant. In contrast, hybrid varieties may not reliably reproduce the same traits, leading to unpredictable results.

Healthy, productive plants are the best candidates for seed saving. A gardener once made the mistake of saving tomato seeds from a weak, disease-prone plant—only to end up with even weaker seedlings the next year. Since then, he always selects the biggest, healthiest specimens for seed saving, ensuring that each generation improves.

Saving Seeds from Popular Vegetables

Tomatoes: The process begins by choosing a **fully ripe, healthy fruit**. Cutting it open reveals seeds encased in a gelatinous coating. These seeds need fermentation to remove this coating, which inhibits germination. Placing them in a jar with a bit of water and letting them sit for a few days allows this natural process to happen. Once the mixture develops a slight film, the seeds can be rinsed, dried, and stored.

Peppers: Unlike tomatoes, peppers require no fermentation. Simply scooping out the seeds from a fully mature, deep-colored fruit, drying them on a paper towel, and storing them in a cool, dark place ensures a good supply for next season.

Beans & Peas: These are among the easiest seeds to save. Allowing pods to dry completely on the plant ensures the seeds inside are fully mature. Once the pods turn brown and brittle, they can be collected, shelled, and stored in an airtight container.

Cucumbers & Squash: Like tomatoes, these seeds need fermentation. Selecting an **overripe fruit** (far past its usual harvesting stage) provides the most viable seeds. After scooping them out, a quick fermentation process ensures they remain viable and free of disease.

Lettuce & Herbs: These plants often "bolt" (send up flower stalks) in hot weather. Once the flowers dry, they form tiny seeds that can be shaken into a paper bag and stored. Basil, cilantro, and dill all follow a similar pattern, offering an abundance of seeds with almost no effort.

A frugal gardener once turned a single packet of lettuce seeds into a perpetual supply simply by allowing a few plants to bolt each year. With just a little patience, he never had to buy lettuce seeds again.

Storing Seeds for Maximum Longevity

After harvesting, seeds must be fully dry before storage. Any moisture can cause mold or premature sprouting. Storing seeds in paper envelopes, glass jars, or resealable bags in a cool, dry place ensures they last as long as possible. Some gardeners even store seeds in the refrigerator or freezer for extended viability.

Labeling is key—many seeds look alike, and a forgotten label can lead to surprises in the next planting season. A well-organized seed collection quickly becomes one of the most valuable resources in a frugal garden.

PERENNIAL PROPAGATION: EXPANDING THE GARDEN FOR FREE

While annuals require replanting each year, perennials return season after season, making them a smart investment for the money-saving gardener. Many can be multiplied through simple propagation techniques, allowing a single plant to turn into a thriving patch without spending a cent.

The Best Perennials to Propagate in Late Summer

Many perennials respond well to propagation in **late summer or early fall**, when the weather is warm but not too harsh.

- **Berry Bushes (Raspberries, Blackberries, Blueberries)**: Cane berries like raspberries and blackberries send out new shoots

(suckers) that can be dug up and replanted. Blueberries, while slower to propagate, can be divided or rooted from cuttings.
- **Herbs (Mint, Oregano, Thyme, Chives, Lemon Balm)**: Many herbs spread naturally and can be divided easily. A gardener once expanded her herb garden by simply splitting clumps of chives and replanting them in different areas—a free way to fill every garden bed with fresh, fragrant herbs.
- **Strawberries**: These plants send out **runners**, which are essentially baby plants. Pinning these runners down into the soil allows them to root, creating new strawberry plants at no cost.
- **Rhubarb & Asparagus**: These long-lived vegetables benefit from division every few years. Cutting a mature rhubarb crown into sections and replanting them extends the harvest for decades.

How to Propagate Perennials with Simple Techniques

One of the simplest ways to multiply perennials is division—digging up an established plant and splitting it into smaller sections, each with its own root system. This works especially well for herbs, daylilies, and rhubarb.

Another method is cuttings, where a portion of the plant (often a stem or root) is removed and encouraged to grow new roots. A gardener once filled an entire backyard with free lavender plants by simply snipping healthy stems, dipping them in rooting hormone, and planting them in moist soil. Within weeks, each cutting developed roots, growing into a lush lavender hedge at no cost.

For woody perennials like grapes, elderberries, and figs, layering works well. This involves bending a low-growing branch to the ground, burying part of it in soil, and waiting for roots to form. Once rooted, the new plant can be separated from the parent and transplanted elsewhere.

A Self-Sustaining Garden Without the Costs

A garden that replenishes itself each year—through seed saving and perennial propagation—removes the need for costly plant purchases and seed orders. A small collection of well-tended perennials can expand into a full garden in just a few seasons, while a habit of saving seeds ensures a steady supply of vegetables year after year.

A truly money-saving garden doesn't just grow food—it grows itself, allowing a gardener to enjoy an abundant harvest with minimal investment. By embracing seed saving and propagation, even the smallest garden can become a self-sustaining, ever-expanding source of food and beauty—all for free.

PROPAGATING FRUIT TREES AND BERRY BUSHES FROM CUTTINGS

Buying fruit trees and berry bushes can be expensive, but with the right techniques, a gardener can multiply their plants for free. Propagating from cuttings allows for the cloning of favorite fruit varieties, ensuring that the new plants produce the same high-quality fruit as the original.

Many experienced gardeners have built entire orchards from a handful of cuttings, simply by taking advantage of the natural ability of plants to regenerate. A single fig tree or grapevine can yield dozens of new plants, and a well-pruned raspberry bush can provide an endless supply of cuttings. With patience and the right methods, any gardener can expand their fruit production without spending a dime.

The Best Fruit Plants to Propagate from Cuttings

Not all fruit trees and berry bushes are easy to propagate from cuttings, but many **root readily with minimal effort**. Some of the easiest and most successful include:

- **Berry Bushes:** Blackberries, raspberries, elderberries, currants, and gooseberries.
- **Grapevines:** Root easily from hardwood or softwood cuttings.
- **Fig Trees:** One of the most foolproof fruit trees to propagate.
- **Mulberries:** Can be rooted from dormant hardwood cuttings.
- **Pomegranates:** Thrive when propagated from summer cuttings.

While apples, pears, peaches, and plums are traditionally grown from **grafted stock**, they can also be propagated from cuttings, though they may take longer to bear fruit and may not be as productive as grafted trees.

How to Propagate Fruit Trees and Berry Bushes from Cuttings

Choosing the Right Type of Cutting

The success of propagation depends largely on the **type of cutting** used. There are two main options:

- **Softwood Cuttings (Spring-Early Summer):** These come from new, flexible growth and root quickly, but they require **high humidity** to prevent drying out. Best for elderberries, figs, and grapes.
- **Hardwood Cuttings (Late Fall-Winter):** Taken from dormant, mature wood, these take longer to root but are more **resilient**. Best for mulberries, currants, and gooseberries.

Step-by-Step Guide to Propagating from Cuttings

1. **Take a Healthy Cutting**
    - Using clean, sharp pruners, cut a **6-12 inch section** of branch.
    - Choose a stem about the thickness of a pencil, as thinner or thicker stems often fail to root.

- Remove any flowers or fruit to direct energy into root growth.
2. **Prepare the Cutting**
   - Strip the lower leaves from the cutting to expose the nodes where roots will form.
   - Make a clean, diagonal cut at the base to maximize the surface area for rooting.
   - Dip the cut end in rooting hormone (optional, but it speeds up root development).
3. **Plant the Cutting**
   - Place the cutting in a pot filled with moist sand, perlite, or light compost.
   - Water gently and cover with a plastic bag or humidity dome to retain moisture.
4. **Provide the Right Conditions**
   - Softwood cuttings need warmth (70°F) and indirect light.
   - Hardwood cuttings should be kept cool and slightly damp until roots form.
5. **Transplant Once Rooted**
   - After **4-8 weeks**, gently tug the cutting—if there's resistance, roots have formed.
   - Transplant into a larger pot or directly into the garden.

An Orchard from Cuttings: A Gardener's Success Story

A gardener once started with a single elderberry bush, knowing how valuable the berries were for homemade syrups and teas. Each spring, he took softwood cuttings, planting them in small containers under a shade cloth. Within a few months, almost every cutting had rooted. By the end of the season, he had enough young elderberry bushes to create a dense hedge—all for free.

Another gardener, after pruning her grapevine, saved the discarded trimmings and stuck them in the ground as an experiment. She forgot about them until the following spring, when she was surprised to see new leaves emerging. That year, she trained the new vines along a trellis, turning her cuttings into productive grapevines without any cost.

HOW TO STORE SEEDS FOR MAXIMUM VIABILITY

Saving seeds is one of the most powerful ways to cut gardening costs, but storing them properly is essential to ensure they remain viable for future planting. Seeds are living embryos, and while they can last for years, exposure to moisture, heat, and light can significantly reduce their ability to germinate. Proper storage techniques can turn a single season's harvest into a long-term seed bank, ensuring a continuous supply of plants without the need for costly seed purchases.

Many experienced gardeners have learned the value of seed storage the hard way. One gardener, eager to save seeds from a particularly flavorful heirloom tomato, simply tossed them into an open jar on a sunny windowsill. The following spring, none of them sprouted. It was a lesson in how improper storage can render even the best seeds useless. Since then, they carefully dry, label, and store their seeds in a cool, dark place, ensuring reliable germination year after year.

Key Factors for Seed Viability

The longevity of seeds depends on three critical factors: moisture, temperature, and light. Excess moisture can cause mold or premature sprouting, while exposure to heat and light can break down the seed's protective coatings and essential nutrients. Keeping seeds dry, cool, and dark extends their viability, sometimes for decades.

After harvesting, seeds should be thoroughly dried to prevent mold. A well-ventilated room with low humidity works best. Some gardeners spread seeds on paper towels or mesh screens for a few weeks, ensuring they are completely dry before storage. Placing damp seeds into storage containers too soon is a common mistake that leads to disappointing results when planting time comes.

Best Storage Methods for Long-Term Viability

Once dry, seeds should be stored in airtight containers to protect them from humidity. Glass jars, resealable plastic bags, or even vacuum-sealed pouches work well. Adding a small packet of silica gel or a pinch of dry rice helps absorb any remaining moisture, preventing rot and mold.

Temperature is another key factor. Seeds last longest when stored in a **cool** location—ideally between 32–50°F (0–10°C). A basement, root cellar, or refrigerator is ideal, as long as the seeds are protected from condensation. Freezing can extend viability for many seeds, but sudden temperature changes should be avoided. When removing frozen seeds for planting, allowing them to slowly come to room temperature before opening the container prevents moisture from condensing on them.

Proper labeling is crucial. Every gardener, at some point, has opened a mystery bag of seeds, unsure of what they saved the previous year. Using envelopes, jars, or seed packets with clear labels—including plant variety, harvest date, and any notes on germination success—prevents confusion and helps track viability over time.

How Long Can Seeds Last?

Some seeds remain viable for only a year or two, while others can last decades if stored properly. Onion, parsley, and corn seeds tend to lose viability quickly, while beans, tomatoes, and squash can last five years or more. A gardener once planted a 20-year-old lettuce seed found in an old envelope and was surprised when it still germinated. While this isn't the norm, it shows that proper storage can preserve seeds for much longer than expected.

Testing stored seeds before planting can save time and frustration. A simple germination test—placing a few seeds between damp paper towels and keeping them warm for a few days—reveals whether they are still viable. If fewer than half sprout, planting extra seeds or sourcing fresh ones might be necessary.

A Seed Bank for the Future

Storing seeds properly not only saves money but also allows gardeners to cultivate plants adapted to their local climate and soil conditions. Over time, saved seeds can become stronger and more resilient, producing better harvests with each passing year. By mastering seed storage techniques, any gardener can ensure a reliable, self-sustaining seed supply, eliminating the need to buy new packets every spring.

BUDGET-FRIENDLY WAYS TO PREPARE FOR THE FALL GARDEN

As summer crops wind down, preparing for the fall garden is one of the smartest ways to extend the growing season while keeping costs low. Many gardeners make the mistake of assuming that gardening ends in late summer, but with the right planning, fall can be just as productive—often with less work and fewer pests.

A frugal gardener once transformed their backyard into a near year-round food source simply by taking advantage of the cooler months. Instead of pulling up spent summer crops and leaving the soil bare, they sowed spinach, carrots, and garlic, ensuring fresh harvests well into winter. With a little foresight and the right techniques, any gardener can prepare for fall without spending extra money.

Using Existing Resources for Fall Planting

Many seeds needed for fall planting are already on hand from earlier in the season. Instead of purchasing new packets, checking seed inventories first can reveal leftover lettuce, kale, or radish seeds that thrive in cooler temperatures. Since fall gardens often require fewer pest treatments, even small amounts of leftover seeds can go a long way.

Soil preparation is another essential step, but it doesn't have to be costly. Rather than buying expensive compost or fertilizers, many gardeners revitalize soil using **grass clippings, aged leaves, or homemade compost**. A layer of mulch from shredded paper or straw helps retain moisture and insulate young seedlings against temperature fluctuations.

For those who need to improve soil structure quickly, cover cropping is a cost-effective solution. Clover, mustard, and winter rye can be sown in empty beds to fix nitrogen, suppress weeds, and prevent soil erosion—all for just a few dollars or even for free if seeds are collected from previous plantings.

Repurposing Summer Crops for Fall Protection

Old summer plants can serve new purposes in a fall garden. Tomato cages and bean trellises can be reused to support fall peas or vining squashes. Corn stalks, often discarded after harvest, can serve as windbreaks for more delicate fall crops.

A gardener once left a few sunflowers standing through autumn, only to discover that they provided **natural frost protection** for the greens growing beneath them. The large stalks helped trap heat at night, creating a microclimate that extended the growing season without the need for row covers or expensive cold frames.

Extending the Growing Season on a Budget

Protecting fall crops from unexpected frosts can be done without buying expensive greenhouses or row covers. Old bedsheets, plastic containers, or even **recycled milk jugs** can be repurposed into makeshift frost protection. Placing clear plastic or glass over low-growing crops creates an inexpensive cold frame, allowing harvests to continue even as temperatures drop.

For gardeners looking to invest in long-term solutions, DIY hoop houses made from **PVC pipes and plastic sheeting** are one of the most affordable ways to extend the season. Many fall greens, such as spinach and Swiss chard, can survive well into winter with just a little added protection.

A Fall Garden That Pays for Itself

Planning a fall garden with frugality in mind allows gardeners to make the most of the growing season without extra expenses. By using saved seeds, enriching soil with free amendments, and repurposing summer structures, a productive fall garden can be established with little to no cost.

A well-prepared fall garden not only provides fresh vegetables when grocery prices peak but also improves soil health for the following year. With careful planning and resourcefulness, even the smallest backyard plot can yield harvests deep into the colder months—proving that a thriving, money-saving garden doesn't end with summer.

CHAPTER 9

SEPTEMBER: FREE FERTILIZERS & FALL PREP

As summer fades, September marks the transition from peak harvests to preparing the garden for colder months. Many gardeners make the mistake of thinking fall is a time to wind down, but in reality, it's one of the most important times to build soil fertility and ensure a strong start for next year's crops.

Rather than relying on expensive store-bought fertilizers, a money-saving gardener takes advantage of free, homemade alternatives to enrich the soil. Organic compost teas, nutrient-rich mulches, and strategic soil amendments can rejuvenate tired garden beds without extra cost. With the right approach, fall preparation can set the stage for healthier plants, fewer pests, and bigger harvests in the following seasons—all while keeping expenses low.

DIY ORGANIC COMPOST TEAS FOR SOIL HEALTH

Compost tea is one of the most powerful and cost-effective ways to boost soil fertility, improve plant health, and enhance microbial life in the garden. Unlike expensive liquid fertilizers, compost tea is essentially a nutrient-rich "brew" made from decomposed organic matter. When applied to the soil or used as a foliar spray, it delivers beneficial microbes, essential nutrients, and natural disease resistance—all for free.

A gardener once struggled with poor soil and weak plants despite adding compost every season. After experimenting with compost tea, they saw a dramatic improvement—plants became more vigorous, soil texture improved, and pest problems decreased. The reason? Compost tea provides instant bioavailable nutrients that plants can absorb immediately, unlike solid compost, which takes longer to break down.

How to Make Compost Tea for Free

Making compost tea is incredibly simple and requires only a few basic materials:

1. **Start with high-quality compost** – Homemade compost is best, but worm castings or aged manure can also be used.
2. **Fill a bucket with water** – Rainwater is ideal, but tap water should be left to sit for 24 hours to allow chlorine to evaporate.
3. **Add compost to a porous bag (or directly into the water)** – An old pillowcase, mesh bag, or even pantyhose works well to contain the compost.
4. **Steep for 24–48 hours** – Stir occasionally to encourage oxygen flow, or use an aquarium pump for aeration.
5. **Apply to the garden** – Use the finished tea as a root drench or foliar spray, straining it first if using a sprayer.

The beauty of compost tea is that it **costs nothing** yet provides incredible benefits. It improves soil structure, boosts plant immunity, and enhances nutrient uptake—all essential for a thriving, self-sustaining garden.

Other Free Fertilizers for Fall Prep

While compost tea is an excellent liquid feed, solid soil amendments also play a vital role in rebuilding nutrients before winter. Many of these fertilizers can be gathered, made, or repurposed from existing resources, eliminating the need for store-bought solutions.

One of the best free fertilizers is leaf mold—decomposed leaves that add organic matter and beneficial fungi to the soil. Instead of bagging and discarding autumn leaves, many gardeners rake them directly onto garden beds or compost them to create a rich, natural soil conditioner.

Another hidden resource is diluted urine, which contains nitrogen, phosphorus, and potassium in an instantly available form. Mixed at a 10:1 ratio with water, it becomes a potent (and completely free) fertilizer that rivals commercial products. Many historical gardens thrived on human waste, long before synthetic fertilizers became widespread.

For those with livestock or access to local farms, aged manure from chickens, cows, or rabbits is a powerful addition to fall soil prep. Unlike synthetic fertilizers, manure improves soil texture, retains moisture, and promotes beneficial microbial activity. Even kitchen scraps, like banana peels and eggshells, can be directly buried in garden beds, slowly releasing potassium and calcium over time.

A gardener who once relied on costly fertilizers discovered that by layering grass clippings, compost, and autumn leaves, their soil became richer and more productive than ever before—without spending a cent. Nature provides everything needed for soil health; it's simply a matter of using resources wisely.

Preparing Garden Beds for Fall and Beyond

Once the garden has been fed with nutrient-rich teas and amendments, proper soil protection is key. Many gardeners make the mistake of leaving beds bare over winter, leading to erosion, nutrient loss, and compacted soil. Instead, cover crops, mulch, and strategic planting can protect and build soil for next year's success.

One of the most frugal yet effective methods is planting cover crops like clover, mustard, or winter rye. These "green manures" fix nitrogen in the soil, prevent weed growth, and improve soil structure—all without requiring expensive inputs. In the spring, they can be tilled under or used as mulch, adding even more organic matter.

For those who prefer a low-maintenance approach, deep mulching with free materials such as straw, shredded newspaper, or wood chips can insulate the soil and retain moisture through the colder months. Some gardeners have successfully overwintered root crops like carrots and beets simply by covering them with a thick layer of leaves or straw, allowing for fresh harvests well into winter.

Another overlooked strategy is leaving certain plants in place rather than pulling them up entirely. The roots of peas, beans, and other nitrogen-fixing plants continue to nourish the soil even after they stop producing. A gardener who let their pea vines decompose directly in the soil found that their spring-planted crops grew stronger and healthier without additional fertilizers.

A Garden That Replenishes Itself for Free

Fall preparation doesn't have to be expensive. By using homemade compost teas, natural fertilizers, and soil-building techniques, gardeners can replenish nutrients, improve soil health, and set the stage for next year's growth—all without spending extra money.

A truly self-sustaining garden isn't built on expensive products but on resourcefulness and nature's own cycles. With a little planning and creativity, every gardener can enter the next growing season with healthier soil, stronger plants, and a more abundant harvest—without ever reaching for their wallet.

COLLECTING AND USING LEAF MOLD: NATURE'S FREE MULCH

As autumn arrives, trees shed their leaves in a natural cycle that enriches the soil. Many gardeners see fallen leaves as a nuisance to be raked and discarded, but experienced growers know that leaves are one of the most valuable and **completely free** resources for improving soil health. When properly collected and broken down, they transform into leaf mold—a rich, humus-like material that enhances moisture retention, adds organic matter, and boosts beneficial microbial activity in garden beds.

A gardener once struggled with dry, sandy soil that refused to hold moisture. Instead of investing in expensive soil amendments, they gathered leaves from their yard and neighbors, piling them in a corner of the garden. A year later, what was once dry, lifeless dirt had become dark, moisture-rich earth. Leaf mold had worked its magic, proving that nature provides everything a gardener needs—without a price tag.

To create leaf mold, simply collect leaves in a pile or a ventilated bin and let them break down over time. Unlike traditional compost, leaf mold decomposes mainly through fungal activity rather than bacterial heat, making the process slower but equally beneficial. Leaves should be kept moist and turned occasionally to encourage decomposition. Depending on climate and leaf type, it can take anywhere from six months to two years for leaves to fully break down into crumbly, dark leaf mold.

Using leaf mold in the garden is simple. As a mulch, it insulates soil, conserves water, and suppresses weeds. When incorporated into planting beds, it improves soil structure, making heavy clay more workable and helping sandy soil retain nutrients. It's also an excellent addition to compost piles, balancing high-nitrogen materials like grass clippings. Some gardeners even use leaf mold as a potting mix component, reducing the need for costly store-bought blends.

The best part is that leaf mold is entirely free. Many cities collect and dispose of leaves in the fall, but savvy gardeners take advantage of this overlooked resource, gathering bagged leaves from curbsides or local parks. With a little patience, what others see as waste becomes one of the most valuable soil conditioners available—proving once again that the best gardening resources don't have to cost a thing.

BEST FREE AND CHEAP COVER CROPS FOR SOIL IMPROVEMENT

Leaving garden beds bare over winter is one of the quickest ways to lose soil fertility. Rain, wind, and temperature fluctuations strip nutrients and cause erosion, undoing months of careful cultivation. Cover crops offer a simple, budget-friendly solution. These fast-growing plants protect the soil, suppress weeds, and improve fertility, all while requiring little to no investment.

A frugal gardener who once struggled with depleted soil discovered the power of cover crops by accident. After letting clover grow unchecked in an unused bed, they found the soil rich and loose the following spring. From then on, they embraced cover cropping as a free way to nourish the garden without relying on expensive fertilizers.

The best cover crops depend on climate and soil needs, but several varieties are easy to grow and cost little or nothing. White clover, often found in lawns, fixes nitrogen and creates a living mulch. Mustard greens suppress nematodes and break up compacted soil. Winter rye, a hardy cereal grain, grows quickly and adds biomass when tilled under.

For those looking to source cover crop seeds on a budget, many feed stores sell bulk grains like oats and rye at a fraction of the price of specialty garden seeds. Farmers often use these crops for livestock feed, but they work just as well in the home garden. Some gardeners even collect seeds from previous plantings, allowing them to sow year after year without additional cost.

Sowing cover crops is simple. Seeds can be broadcast over empty beds in late summer or early fall, raked in lightly, and left to grow until spring. When it's time to plant, they can be tilled under as green manure or cut and left as mulch, enriching the soil without needing store-bought compost or fertilizers.

SMART END-OF-SEASON SEED SWAPS

As the growing season winds down, many gardeners find themselves with an abundance of extra seeds—whether from saved crops, leftover seed packets, or self-seeding plants. Rather than letting these seeds go to waste or spending money on new ones next year, participating in a **seed swap** is one of the smartest and most frugal ways to expand a garden without spending a dime.

A gardener once walked into a seed swap event with only a handful of marigold seeds and a few extras from last season's squash. They left with heirloom tomatoes, rare herbs, and an entire selection of greens—seeds that would have cost a fortune if bought individually. More importantly, they gained knowledge from seasoned growers, learning tips about each variety's best-growing conditions.

Seed swaps come in many forms. Some are formal events organized by gardening groups, community centers, or libraries, while others are informal gatherings among friends. Online gardening communities also offer seed exchange programs where growers can mail small quantities to each other. These swaps allow gardeners to access regionally adapted seeds that are often **better suited to local climates** than commercial varieties.

For those who don't have an organized seed swap nearby, starting one is easy. A few gardeners can simply agree to trade their extra seeds, ensuring that everyone gets something new to try in the next growing season. Even unexpected places—workplaces, social clubs, or neighborhood groups—can serve as great starting points for building a community of resourceful, cost-conscious growers.

The key to a successful seed swap is proper labeling and seed viability. Seeds should be stored in cool, dry places, labeled with variety names and collection dates, and checked for quality. Sharing knowledge about germination rates and preferred growing conditions makes swaps even more valuable.

In the end, a simple seed swap is more than just an exchange of seeds—it's an exchange of knowledge, experience, and community connections. It keeps gardening accessible to all, preserves heirloom varieties, and ensures that gardeners are never reliant on expensive seed companies for their next harvest.

PREPARING A NO-COST COMPOST PILE FOR WINTER

Many gardeners mistakenly believe that composting is only a warm-weather activity, but in reality, fall and winter composting can be one of the best ways to prepare for next season's success. While decomposition slows in cold temperatures, the organic matter continues to break down, and by spring, the pile will be rich, dark, and ready to nourish garden beds. Best of all, it requires no costly additives or equipment—just natural materials and a little patience.

One gardener, determined to garden on a tight budget, started composting with nothing but a simple pile of autumn leaves and kitchen scraps. Without a fancy compost bin or store-bought accelerators, they let nature do the work. By the time spring arrived, their compost was filled with nutrient-rich humus, proving that expensive composting systems are not a necessity—just a convenience.

Creating a no-cost compost pile is simple. Start by choosing a spot in the garden that allows for airflow and drainage. It doesn't need to be enclosed—a simple heap on the ground will work just as well as a commercial bin. Layer carbon-rich "browns" (leaves, straw, shredded paper) with nitrogen-rich "greens" (vegetable scraps, coffee grounds, garden trimmings), ensuring a good balance for decomposition. Turning the pile occasionally will speed up the process, but even without frequent turning, decomposition will occur over time.

Some gardeners use trench composting, a method where kitchen scraps are buried directly in garden beds over winter. By spring, the buried material has broken down into nutrient-rich compost right where the plants will need it, eliminating the need to transfer finished compost later.

For those who want to speed up winter composting, insulating the pile with a thick layer of straw, leaves, or even cardboard can help retain heat and keep microbes active. Some gardeners place a black tarp over their compost to absorb heat from the sun, keeping decomposition steady even in cold weather.

Regardless of the method used, composting through the winter ensures that when spring arrives, nutrient-rich, homemade compost will be ready to feed garden beds—without a single dollar spent on bagged fertilizers or store-bought soil amendments.

A Garden That Gives Back

Both seed swapping and composting embody the spirit of a truly sustainable, money-saving garden. By participating in seed exchanges, gardeners expand their plant varieties for free while preserving valuable heirloom seeds. By composting through the winter, they turn waste into nourishment, ensuring that next season's plants will grow in soil that is naturally rich and fertile.

Ultimately, a frugal gardener understands that nature already provides everything needed for abundance—it's just a matter of using resources wisely. Through simple, cost-free practices like these, every garden can be both productive and financially sustainable, ensuring bigger harvests, healthier soil, and zero unnecessary expenses year after year.

CHAPTER 10

OCTOBER: ECONOMICAL GARDEN CLEAN-UP & SOIL BUILDING

As the growing season winds down, many gardeners see October as a time to clear out the remains of summer crops and put the garden to rest. But a frugal, resourceful gardener knows that fall is not the end—it's the foundation for next year's success. Instead of discarding organic materials or leaving soil bare, October is the perfect month to enrich garden beds using free, natural resources that will build soil health over the winter.

One of the most overlooked yet valuable garden amendments is something that most people rake into piles and throw away—fall leaves. When properly used, they become an abundant, zero-cost resource that improves soil structure, adds organic matter, and feeds beneficial microorganisms.

USING FALL LEAVES TO ENRICH GARDEN BEDS

A gardener once noticed a striking difference in two parts of their yard. One section, regularly raked clean in autumn, struggled with compacted, lifeless soil. The other, where leaves were left to break down naturally, had dark, crumbly earth filled with earthworms. This simple observation changed the way they saw fall leaves—not as yard waste, but as nature's gift to the soil.

Leaves are rich in carbon, trace minerals, and organic matter, making them an excellent addition to garden beds. Left to decompose over winter, they improve soil texture, boost microbial activity, and help retain moisture in the coming growing season.

Ways to Use Fall Leaves in the Garden

1. **Leaf Mulch**: The simplest way to use leaves is as a natural mulch. Spread a thick layer (about 3-6 inches) over garden beds, around perennials, and between rows of fall crops. Over time, the leaves will break down, adding nutrients and protecting the soil from erosion. Shredded leaves break down faster and prevent matting, but even whole leaves will decompose with time.

2. **Leaf Mold for Future Soil Health**: By gathering leaves into a pile or bin and letting them sit for 6-12 months, gardeners can create leaf mold—a soft, humus-like material that retains moisture better than peat moss. This slow-composted material improves soil structure and can be used in potting mixes or added to planting beds in spring.

3. **Lasagna Gardening (Sheet Mulching)**: For gardeners looking to create new beds without digging, fall leaves are a key ingredient in the no-till method known as lasagna gardening. Simply layer cardboard or newspaper over the ground, add leaves, grass clippings, and compost on top, and let it sit over winter. By spring, the layers will have broken down into rich, plant-ready soil.

4. **Composting with Leaves**: Leaves are an excellent brown (carbon) ingredient for compost piles. They balance nitrogen-rich materials like food scraps, garden waste, and grass clippings, preventing compost from becoming too wet or smelly. Mixing in leaves also aerates the pile, ensuring proper decomposition through winter.

5. **Worm Bedding for Vermicomposting**: If using a worm composting system, shredded leaves make a fantastic bedding material. They provide a natural habitat for worms while adding valuable nutrients to worm castings.

Many cities collect and dispose of leaves in fall, but savvy gardeners take advantage of this free bounty. In some neighborhoods, bagged leaves appear on curbsides, free for the taking. Gathering these leaves and using them wisely turns an overlooked resource into one of the most valuable soil-building tools available—without spending a cent.

LOW-COST WAYS TO PROTECT PLANTS FROM FROST

As October brings cooler nights, many gardeners brace for the first frost, often seen as the abrupt end of the growing season. However, with a few simple and affordable techniques, plants can be protected from sudden temperature drops, extending harvests by weeks or even months. Expensive frost covers aren't necessary when resourcefulness comes into play.

A gardener once faced an unexpected frost while their tomato and pepper plants were still full of fruit. Without expensive row covers, they used old bedsheets, overturned buckets, and piles of leaves to shield their crops. To their surprise, most of the plants survived, proving that frost protection doesn't have to be costly—it simply requires creativity and an understanding of how to trap warmth.

The key to frost protection is insulation. Trapping heat around plants keeps ice crystals from forming inside their cells, preventing damage. Many everyday household items serve this purpose. Old sheets, blankets, and burlap are excellent for covering plants overnight and should be removed in the morning to allow the sun to reheat the soil.

Placing gallon-sized plastic jugs with the bottoms removed over individual plants creates a mini greenhouse effect. Some gardeners even fill clear bottles with warm water and place them near plants to slowly release heat overnight.

Mulching is another effective, budget-friendly strategy. A thick layer of leaves, straw, or grass clippings around the base of plants insulates the roots and keeps soil temperatures stable. Leaf mulch works particularly well for cold-hardy crops like carrots, kale, and beets. In cases of sudden frost warnings, upturned buckets, flower pots, or even cardboard boxes provide a quick solution for covering plants, especially when weighted down to prevent them from blowing away.

Water also acts as a natural heat source. Large buckets or jugs filled with water placed near plants absorb heat during the day and slowly release it at night, creating a buffer against cold air. More advanced yet still affordable solutions include mini hoop houses made from flexible PVC pipes or metal wire, covered with plastic sheeting or old shower curtains. These makeshift tunnels function like small greenhouses, offering long-term protection against frost, wind, and even early snowfall.

By using these low-cost and often free methods, gardeners can continue harvesting well into late fall or even winter. Extending the season doesn't require expensive products—just an understanding of how to work with available materials to maximize natural warmth and insulation.

MAKING COLD FRAMES FROM SALVAGED WINDOWS

A cold frame is one of the simplest ways to extend the growing season. It acts like a miniature greenhouse, protecting plants from frost while allowing sunlight to warm the soil. Cold frames are especially useful for hardening off seedlings, overwintering greens, and keeping the soil workable longer into the season.

One gardener, determined to build a cold frame without spending a dime, scavenged old windows from a demolition site. Using salvaged bricks, scrap wood, and a few nails, they built a fully functional cold frame that kept lettuce and spinach thriving into November. This experience reinforced the idea that extending the growing season doesn't have to be expensive—resourcefulness is often more valuable than money.

To build a DIY cold frame, the first step is to find old windows or clear panels. These can often be sourced for free from yard sales, thrift stores, or even online marketplaces where people discard old storm windows or picture frames. Once the windows are secured, a base needs to be constructed. Scrap wood, bricks, cinder blocks, or even straw bales work well. The back wall should be higher than the front so the window panel slopes downward, allowing rain to run off while maximizing sun exposure.

The salvaged window serves as the lid and should be hinged or easily removable so it can be propped open on warm days and closed at night for insulation. Proper positioning is crucial—placing the cold frame in a south-facing spot ensures it receives the most sunlight. Additional insulation can be added by lining the inner walls with straw bales or thick cardboard. Some gardeners place jugs of water inside the frame to absorb heat during the day and release it at night, further protecting plants from frost.

Cold frames are particularly useful for growing leafy greens like lettuce, spinach, and kale, as well as root crops such as carrots and radishes. They also help in starting early spring seedlings before transplanting them outdoors.

By repurposing salvaged materials, a cold frame can be built for little to no cost, offering an effective way to keep fresh food growing long after the first frost. Instead of seeing the colder months as the end of the season, a well-built cold frame allows for continued productivity, proving that gardening doesn't have to stop when temperatures drop.

DIY ROW COVERS FOR SEASON EXTENSION

As temperatures drop, many gardeners assume their growing season is coming to an end. However, with simple and inexpensive row covers, crops can be protected from frost, wind, and even snow, allowing for extended harvests well into fall and early winter. Row covers act as a protective barrier, trapping warmth while still allowing air and moisture to circulate, creating a microclimate that keeps plants growing longer.

A gardener once faced an unusually early frost in mid-October, just as their lettuce, spinach, and carrots were thriving. Instead of losing their crops, they quickly assembled a row cover using wire hoops and an old bedsheet. The plants survived, and that experience proved that with a bit of creativity, anyone can extend their harvest without relying on expensive season-extension products.

Building a DIY row cover is straightforward. The first step is creating a simple frame using flexible materials like PVC pipes, metal wire, or even branches bent into an arch. These supports should be spaced evenly over the garden bed to provide structure for the covering. A variety of inexpensive materials can be used as the cover itself. Lightweight fabric such as old bedsheets or burlap allows air circulation while shielding plants from frost. Clear plastic or shower curtains create a greenhouse effect, trapping heat during the day and insulating plants at night. For added durability, agricultural fabric, often found at farm supply stores, can be reused for several seasons.

The key to effective row covers is proper ventilation. On sunny days, lifting the covers slightly or propping them open prevents overheating while still protecting crops from cold nights. Anchoring the covers with bricks, stones, or even repurposed water bottles filled with soil ensures they remain secure in strong winds.

Row covers are especially beneficial for leafy greens, carrots, beets, and herbs, all of which can continue growing under protection long after unprotected crops have succumbed to frost. Even in the harshest winters, they provide insulation for overwintering plants like garlic and spinach, allowing them to thrive come spring.

For those who want to garden on a budget, row covers are one of the easiest and most effective ways to extend the season. Using salvaged materials and simple assembly methods, gardeners can protect their crops without expensive greenhouses or high-tech equipment, proving that innovation and resourcefulness are often more valuable than a big budget.

STORING ROOT CROPS WITHOUT EXPENSIVE EQUIPMENT

As fall approaches, one of the biggest concerns for gardeners is how to store their root crops without investing in costly refrigeration or storage solutions. Fortunately, nature provides a simple answer: root crops like carrots, potatoes, beets, and turnips are naturally designed to last long periods when stored properly. With a little planning, they can remain fresh for months without requiring energy-intensive refrigeration.

A gardener once harvested a bumper crop of carrots but had no cellar or specialized storage space. Instead of letting them go to waste, they experimented with different low-cost methods—burying some in sand, storing others in a box filled with leaves, and leaving a few in the ground under a thick mulch. To their surprise, all three methods worked, providing fresh carrots well into winter.

One of the easiest and most traditional ways to store root vegetables is keeping them **in the ground**. By covering the crop with a thick layer of straw, dried leaves, or wood chips, the soil remains insulated, preventing it from freezing. When vegetables are needed, they can simply be dug up as fresh as the day they were harvested. This works particularly well for carrots, parsnips, and beets.

For those who prefer to harvest their crops all at once, an indoor root storage method is essential. The best location for storing root vegetables is a cool, dark place with high humidity—an unheated basement, garage, or even a closet can work if conditions are right. One effective technique is storing root crops in containers filled with moist sand, sawdust, or shredded newspaper. This keeps them from drying out and mimics the conditions of underground storage. Carrots and beets can be layered in a box of damp sand, while potatoes store best in burlap sacks in a dark, well-ventilated space.

Another budget-friendly option is creating a **makeshift root cellar** using a buried container. A simple approach involves taking a large plastic bin or metal trash can, placing it in the ground with the lid just above soil level, and filling it with root vegetables layered in straw or sand. The earth acts as natural insulation, keeping the temperature stable and preventing freezing.

CHAPTER 11

NOVEMBER: EXTENDING THE HARVEST & PREPPING FOR WINTER

As the days grow shorter and temperatures drop, many gardeners assume the growing season is over. However, with the right techniques, it's possible to keep harvesting well into winter—or set the stage for an even more productive spring. November is a time for both preservation and preparation: protecting plants from harsh weather, extending the harvest with insulation techniques, and ensuring the soil remains rich and fertile for the next season.

One of the most cost-effective ways to maintain a productive garden during this time is by insulating raised beds. Raised beds cool down faster than in-ground gardens, but with a few simple and inexpensive adjustments, they can continue to provide fresh greens and root vegetables long after the first frost.

CHEAP & EASY WAYS TO INSULATE RAISED BEDS

Raised beds offer many advantages, from improved drainage to better soil structure, but their elevated nature also makes them more vulnerable to temperature swings. When cold air moves across the garden, it seeps into the sides of raised beds, chilling the soil faster than it would in an in-ground garden. Fortunately, insulation methods can be both simple and budget-friendly.

One of the most effective ways to insulate raised beds is by adding a thick layer of mulch. Leaves, straw, pine needles, and even shredded newspaper can be piled up around the plants, covering the soil to trap warmth. This method works especially well for overwintering carrots, beets, and parsnips, which can be harvested fresh throughout winter simply by pulling back the mulch.

For even greater insulation, the outside of the raised bed itself can be covered with natural materials. Stacking straw bales around the perimeter creates a thick barrier against cold winds. Alternatively, wrapping the sides of the bed with old blankets, burlap sacks, or bubble wrap can slow heat loss, helping the soil retain warmth longer. Some gardeners even place water jugs or bricks along the edges of raised beds—these materials absorb heat during the day and gradually release it at night, providing natural temperature regulation.

For those looking to maximize warmth, adding a **plastic cover or mini hoop house** over a raised bed can transform it into a season-extending powerhouse. Using flexible PVC pipes or wire hoops, gardeners can drape clear plastic or an old shower curtain over the bed, securing the edges with bricks or boards. On sunny days, opening the cover prevents overheating, while at night, closing it traps warmth, keeping crops like spinach, kale, and lettuce thriving even as frost settles in.

Another clever technique is the **hot composting method**, which uses natural decomposition to generate heat. By placing fresh compost materials—such as grass clippings, leaves, and kitchen scraps—along the sides of a raised bed or even layering them beneath the soil before planting, the slow breakdown of organic matter releases warmth, insulating the roots of cold-hardy crops.

With these simple, low-cost insulation strategies, raised beds can continue producing well into the colder months. By making use of free and repurposed materials, gardeners can protect their soil, extend their harvests, and set themselves up for a thriving spring without the expense of heated greenhouses or commercial cold frames.

HOW TO BUILD A LOW-COST WINTER GREENS GARDEN

Growing fresh greens in winter doesn't require a heated greenhouse or expensive equipment. With a little planning and resourcefulness, a budget-friendly winter garden can provide a steady supply of spinach, kale, mache (corn salad), and even lettuce well into the cold months. Many traditional gardeners pack up their tools after the first frost, but those who know how to harness simple season-extension techniques can enjoy fresh, homegrown food year-round.

The first step in building a low-cost winter greens garden is choosing the right location. A south-facing wall, the side of a shed, or any area that receives ample winter sun will help maximize warmth. Raised beds or containers placed against a sun-warmed structure create a microclimate that can keep soil temperatures stable, even in freezing weather.

Once a location is chosen, seasonal protection is key. One of the most cost-effective ways to shield plants from cold temperatures is using row covers or mini hoop houses. These can be built using flexible PVC pipes, metal wire, or even repurposed branches bent into arches over the garden bed. Covering these frames with clear plastic sheeting, old shower curtains, or even discarded window panes creates a simple greenhouse effect, trapping warmth during the day and insulating plants at night.

For those who want an even simpler approach, cold frames—essentially mini greenhouses made from salvaged materials—are an excellent option. Old windows placed atop straw-bale walls or wooden frames create a protective barrier against frost while still allowing sunlight to warm the soil. Some gardeners bury large storage bins or wooden boxes slightly underground and cover them with glass or plastic to create an affordable underground cold frame.

In especially cold regions, **a layered protection method** can be highly effective. First, a thick layer of mulch—such as straw, dried leaves, or shredded newspaper—acts as insulation around the plants. On top of that, a row cover or plastic sheet traps warmth. Some gardeners go even further by placing plastic bottles filled with water inside their covered beds. These bottles absorb heat during the day and slowly release it at night, creating a natural heat source.

When selecting crops, choosing **cold-hardy greens** is essential. Spinach, mache, kale, and mustard greens not only tolerate frost but actually become sweeter after exposure to cold temperatures. These plants thrive with minimal care and can be harvested continuously throughout winter.

A winter greens garden proves that fresh, nutritious food doesn't have to stop when summer ends. By making use of repurposed materials, natural insulation, and smart planting techniques, gardeners can enjoy homegrown produce even in the coldest months—without spending a fortune.

MAKING HOMEMADE POTTING SOIL FOR NEXT YEAR

Buying commercial potting soil every year can be costly, but creating a nutrient-rich homemade mix is not only more affordable—it often results in healthier, more resilient plants. The key to a good potting mix is balancing three essential components: **structure, moisture retention, and nutrients**. By using materials readily available in the garden and home, anyone can create high-quality soil for seedlings, container plants, and raised beds at a fraction of the cost.

The foundation of any potting mix is aeration and drainage, which can be achieved with materials like coconut coir, leaf mold, or well-aged compost. Coconut coir, often used as a peat moss alternative, is lightweight and holds moisture well, while leaf mold—decomposed autumn leaves—creates a fluffy, rich base that plants love. Those with access to well-aged compost can use it as a core ingredient, providing both structure and a boost of nutrients.

For nutrient content, mixing in homemade compost or worm castings ensures plants receive a slow-release supply of essential minerals. A simple compost bin or worm farm can produce this organic matter year-round. Another budget-friendly addition is wood ash, which provides potassium and helps balance soil pH. Gardeners who grow comfrey or nettles can also dry and crush the leaves into the mix, as these plants naturally accumulate beneficial minerals from deep in the soil.

To enhance drainage and aeration, adding sand, perlite, or crushed eggshells prevents the soil from compacting over time. For those who don't want to buy perlite, alternatives such as crushed charcoal or small pieces of pumice can serve the same purpose.

A basic homemade potting mix recipe includes:

- **2 parts compost or leaf mold** (for nutrients and moisture retention)
- **1 part coconut coir or peat alternative** (for aeration)
- **1 part sand, perlite, or crushed eggshells** (for drainage)

For gardeners preparing ahead for next year, storing homemade potting mix in a **cool, dry place**—such as covered bins or old feed bags—keeps it fresh. Some gardeners even mix in dry amendments like crushed banana peels (for potassium) or used coffee grounds (for nitrogen) so the soil is pre-enriched when planting season arrives.

REUSING AND CLEANING OLD SEED TRAYS & CONTAINERS

Reusing seed trays and containers is one of the simplest and most effective ways to cut gardening costs while reducing waste. Instead of buying new trays each year, properly cleaning and storing old ones ensures they remain in good condition for future plantings. Not only does this save money, but it also prevents the spread of diseases that can linger in leftover soil and organic debris.

At the end of the growing season, seed trays, cell packs, and pots often look worse for wear—covered in dried soil, algae, or even bits of old roots. However, with a little effort, they can be restored and used for years. The first step is to remove any leftover soil and plant debris by shaking them out or using a stiff brush. A quick rinse with water helps loosen any stubborn dirt.

To fully disinfect containers, soaking them in a **natural sanitizing solution** is highly effective. While many gardeners use a diluted bleach solution (one part bleach to nine parts water), a more eco-friendly approach involves soaking trays in a mixture of vinegar and water or scrubbing them with hydrogen peroxide. Both methods kill harmful bacteria, fungi, and mold spores without leaving behind chemical residues. After soaking, trays should be thoroughly rinsed and allowed to dry in the sun, as UV light naturally kills lingering pathogens.

For those looking to expand their collection of seed-starting containers without spending a dime, many household items can be repurposed for seed starting. Yogurt cups, egg cartons, takeout containers, and even toilet paper rolls make excellent biodegradable seed-starting pots. With a few drainage holes poked in the bottom, these makeshift pots function just as well as store-bought versions while keeping unnecessary waste out of landfills.

Once clean and dry, stacking trays and containers neatly in a storage bin or shed ensures they're ready for the next planting season. By taking the time to clean and reuse materials, gardeners save money and contribute to a more sustainable, waste-free gardening practice.

WHAT TO BUY NOW FOR NEXT YEAR AT DEEP DISCOUNTS

November is one of the best times of the year to stock up on gardening supplies at significantly reduced prices. As retailers clear out inventory to make room for holiday merchandise and new spring stock, savvy gardeners can take advantage of deep discounts on essential items. By planning ahead and making strategic purchases now, it's possible to save a substantial amount of money for the next growing season.

One of the best items to buy in November is **seeds**. Many garden centers and online retailers discount their seed stock before introducing fresh inventory in the new year. Since most seeds remain viable for several years when stored properly, buying them at end-of-season prices is a smart way to build a seed bank for the following spring.

Larger items like raised bed kits, trellises, and garden tools also see price reductions as demand drops. End-of-season sales often include wheelbarrows, pruners, shovels, and hoses at a fraction of their peak-season cost. Buying high-quality tools now ensures they're ready when spring arrives, avoiding the need to pay full price when gardening season is in full swing.

Soil amendments and fertilizers—especially bulk compost, manure, and organic soil conditioners—are often discounted at local garden centers before winter. Many nurseries prefer to clear out heavy, bulky products rather than store them over the winter, making this a perfect time to stock up. Similarly, mulch can often be found at reduced prices, allowing gardeners to get ahead on insulating garden beds for winter.

For those interested in extending their growing season, cold frames, row covers, and greenhouse materials are also worth purchasing now. As stores make room for holiday decorations, season-extension products are frequently discounted, making it an ideal time to invest in materials that will keep plants thriving in the colder months.

Another often-overlooked discount category is planters, pots, and seed-starting supplies. Whether looking for large ceramic pots or simple seed trays, many stores significantly reduce prices at the end of the gardening season. Even greenhouses and hydroponic kits see markdowns, making it a great time to invest in indoor growing setups.

CHAPTER 12

DECEMBER: REFLECTION & SMART PLANNING FOR NEXT YEAR

As the gardening year winds down, December offers the perfect opportunity to reflect, take notes, and plan for the season ahead. While the garden may be dormant, this is one of the most valuable months for a resourceful gardener—because careful planning now leads to greater success (and bigger savings) in the future.

A money-saving gardener knows that every lesson learned in the past year—whether a triumph or a mistake—translates into better decision-making next season. By taking time to assess what worked and what didn't, gardeners can refine their strategies, cut unnecessary costs, and invest in practices that provide the greatest returns.

REVIEWING WHAT WORKED & WHAT DIDN'T (Saving Money by Learning)

One of the simplest but most effective habits a frugal gardener can develop is keeping detailed notes. A quick review of the past year's successes and setbacks prevents wasted time and money on failed experiments while reinforcing the best cost-effective strategies.

Start by reflecting on high-performing crops. Which plants produced abundantly with minimal effort? Which required too much space, water, or attention for too little yield? Some crops may have outperformed expectations—like a variety of cherry tomatoes that flourished despite neglect—while others may have struggled, indicating they weren't worth the investment.

Next, consider soil health and amendments. Did homemade compost perform as well as store-bought fertilizers? Were there any signs of nutrient deficiencies? Many gardeners realize they don't need to buy expensive fertilizers once they perfect their own composting system, but this requires observation and adjustment over time.

Pest control methods are another area for review. If companion planting or DIY sprays worked well, those should be continued. If a particular pest wreaked havoc despite efforts to control it, it may be worth rethinking plant placement, introducing beneficial insects earlier, or planting natural repellents like marigolds or garlic.

Reviewing season extension techniques can also lead to savings. If a homemade cold frame or row cover effectively kept greens growing into winter, it might be worth expanding that effort next year. On the other hand, if a purchased frost blanket underperformed, a more budget-friendly approach (such as using old blankets or straw insulation) might be just as effective.

Financially, reviewing garden-related spending is key. Many gardeners don't realize how much they spend on supplies until they look back. Keeping track of costs—seeds, tools, amendments, plant starts—helps identify areas where expenses can be reduced. If buying seedlings was costly, starting more plants from seed next year could be a money-saving goal. If a particular tool was purchased but rarely used, it may not have been a worthwhile investment.

December isn't just a time for looking back; it's also the time to apply these lessons to create a more efficient, productive, and budget-friendly garden in the coming year. The most successful frugal gardeners are those who continually refine their methods, reducing waste, increasing efficiency, and making the most of every resource available.

BUDGET-FRIENDLY GARDEN GIFTS & HOLIDAY PROJECTS

December isn't just a time for reflection—it's also a season of giving. For gardeners who appreciate sustainability and frugality, homemade, garden-inspired gifts can be more meaningful than store-bought presents. Whether sharing preserved harvests, crafting practical garden tools, or making simple nature-based gifts, there are countless ways to spread holiday cheer without breaking the bank.

One of the easiest and most appreciated gifts is homemade herb blends and infused oils. A small jar of homegrown dried basil, rosemary, and thyme makes a thoughtful (and useful) present for any cook. Infused oils, such as rosemary or garlic olive oil, require only a few ingredients but feel luxurious. For a more creative spin, gardeners can mix their own herbal teas using dried chamomile, mint, or lemon balm, packaging them in simple tins or jars with handwritten labels.

Another popular DIY gift is handmade seed packets. Saving seeds from favorite garden plants—whether heirloom tomatoes, zinnias, or herbs—allows gardeners to share a piece of their harvest with friends and family. A few well-labeled seed envelopes, along with instructions for growing, make for a thoughtful and practical gift, especially for those new to gardening.

For a rustic and charming gift, garden markers made from repurposed materials are easy to create. Flat stones painted with plant names, wooden spoons etched with labels, or even upcycled wine corks on skewers make creative and useful plant markers. These small, personalized gifts add a unique touch to any garden.

For those who enjoy crafting, DIY plant pots or planters make excellent gifts. Tin cans wrapped in burlap, painted terracotta pots, or even repurposed teacups can serve as beautiful and functional containers for herbs or succulents. Adding a small plant or pack of seeds makes the gift even more special.

Gardeners with an abundance of dried flowers can create botanical sachets, pressed flower bookmarks, or herbal bath salts. Lavender sachets bring a calming scent to closets and drawers, while pressed flower bookmarks make lovely, nature-inspired gifts for book lovers. Bath salts infused with dried rose petals, mint, or chamomile offer a luxurious, spa-like experience made from simple garden ingredients.

For a practical gift with long-term value, consider assembling a garden journal starter kit. A simple notebook, some hand-drawn garden layouts, a few pressed leaves, and a packet of seeds can encourage recipients to start documenting their gardening experiences.

Even those short on time can create meaningful gifts with minimal effort. A basket of homegrown produce, a jar of homemade jam, or a bottle of infused vinegar can be just as appreciated as any store-bought present. Ultimately, the best garden gifts come from the heart—and often, from the soil.

BEST WINTER READING FOR FRUGAL GARDENERS

Winter is the season when many gardeners trade their trowels for books, using the colder months to absorb new knowledge and inspiration. For frugal gardeners, the best books focus on self-sufficiency, cost-saving techniques, and maximizing yields with minimal investment. Whether learning about soil health, DIY projects, or growing food in small spaces, the right books can transform the way a gardener approaches the next season.

For those interested in self-sufficiency and sustainability, classics like *The Resilient Gardener* by Carol Deppe provide invaluable insights into growing staple crops with minimal inputs. Deppe's emphasis on adaptable gardening techniques makes this a must-read for those looking to produce more of their own food without relying on expensive store-bought amendments.

A fantastic resource for budget-conscious gardeners is The Backyard Homestead by Carleen Madigan. This book outlines how to grow an impressive amount of food—even on a small budget—while covering everything from composting to livestock care.

For those passionate about soil health and composting, Teaming with Microbes by Jeff Lowenfels and Wayne Lewis breaks down the science of organic soil building in an easy-to-understand way. A deeper understanding of soil life can help gardeners reduce the need for costly fertilizers and amendments.

Gardeners interested in creative, low-cost solutions will find inspiration in The Revolutionary Yardscape by Matthew Levesque, which focuses on upcycling and repurposing materials for garden design. Similarly, Free-Range Gardening by Lorraine Johnson challenges traditional rules and encourages a more relaxed, resourceful approach to growing food and flowers.

For those who love DIY projects, The Essential Urban Farmer by Novella Carpenter and Willow Rosenthal offers step-by-step guides to building raised beds, chicken coops, and irrigation systems using salvaged materials. This book is especially useful for those looking to make their gardening setup more efficient and cost-effective.

Finally, for a broad yet practical approach to **low-cost gardening**, Grow More with Less by Vincent Simeone provides straightforward advice on how to save money while increasing productivity in the garden.

Whether curling up by the fire with a well-worn classic or diving into a new guide, winter reading provides an opportunity to refine skills, plan smarter, and dream about next year's abundant (and affordable) harvests.

PLANNING NEXT SEASON'S NO-COST EXPERIMENTS

One of the most rewarding aspects of gardening is experimenting with new techniques, plants, and methods. The best gardeners—especially those who focus on frugality—are always testing ways to grow more food, improve soil, and reduce costs. The off-season is the perfect time to plan these experiments for the coming year, ensuring that each test is both practical and cost-effective.

A great no-cost experiment is testing different seed-starting methods. Instead of buying expensive seed trays and potting mix, gardeners can experiment with homemade soil blocks, repurposed containers, or even direct sowing methods. Winter sowing—where seeds are planted in plastic jugs and left outside to naturally germinate—offers another fascinating (and nearly free) way to start seedlings without expensive grow lights.

Another valuable experiment is comparing homemade vs. store-bought fertilizers. Those with compost piles or access to natural amendments like comfrey tea, banana peel fertilizer, or wood ash can compare their effectiveness against commercial fertilizers. By keeping detailed notes on plant growth, yield, and soil health, gardeners can determine whether homemade solutions provide the same benefits—saving money in the long run.

For those interested in increasing harvests, companion planting experiments can be a fun and informative way to boost productivity. Testing different combinations—like planting basil with tomatoes to improve flavor, or marigolds near squash to deter pests—can reveal which pairings work best in a particular garden. Similarly, trying out different **trellising techniques** for vining crops like cucumbers, peas, or pole beans can help maximize vertical space while reducing disease risks.

Another experiment that costs nothing is **soil-building trials**. Gardeners can test different mulching methods, such as leaf mulch versus grass clippings, to see which retains moisture best and suppresses weeds most effectively. Some might try growing cover crops like clover or winter rye and comparing the results against traditional composting.

Finally, a highly practical experiment is **extending the growing season** without costly equipment. Testing different row cover materials—such as old bed sheets versus commercial frost blankets—or experimenting with passive solar heating techniques in small greenhouses can help determine the most cost-effective ways to grow food longer into the colder months.

WHERE TO GET FREE OR DISCOUNTED SEEDS & PLANTS FOR NEXT YEAR

Seeds and plants are the foundation of any garden, but they don't have to be a major expense. Many gardeners grow entire gardens each year without spending a dime on seeds—simply by sourcing them from free or low-cost resources.

One of the best ways to get free seeds is through **seed swaps**. Many communities, libraries, and gardening groups host events where gardeners can exchange excess seeds. If no local swap is available, online platforms like Seed Savers Exchange or social media gardening groups often facilitate trades by mail. A gardener with extra tomato seeds can trade for lettuce or herb seeds, creating a diverse collection without any cost.

Many public libraries now have seed lending programs, where gardeners "borrow" seeds in the spring and return saved seeds at the end of the season. This encourages biodiversity and ensures that local gardeners always have access to affordable planting materials.

Another excellent source of free seeds is harvesting from store-bought or homegrown produce. Many vegetables—such as peppers, tomatoes, squash, and beans—contain seeds that can be saved and replanted. Similarly, flowers like marigolds, sunflowers, and zinnias produce an abundance of seeds that can be stored for the next season.

For those who prefer starter plants, community plant giveaways and online gardening groups can be great resources. Many gardeners end up with extra seedlings in the spring and are happy to share. Local garden clubs, Facebook groups, and Craigslist often have postings for free or low-cost plants, especially during the peak planting season.

Garden centers and nurseries can also be a surprising source of free or discounted plants. By visiting at the end of the season, gardeners may find clearance racks filled with plants that look a little rough but can often be revived with proper care. Many stores even give away plants that are past their prime but still have life left in them.

For those willing to be resourceful, wild foraging and plant division can provide an abundance of free plants. Many herbs like mint, oregano, and lemon balm spread aggressively and can often be found in excess in other gardeners' yards. Similarly, dividing perennials like rhubarb, chives, or hostas from an established plant can yield multiple new plants without spending a penny.

BONUS SECTION

50+ DIY GARDENING HACKS THAT SAVE MONEY

Gardening doesn't have to be expensive. With creativity and resourcefulness, you can reduce costs while improving productivity. These 50+ DIY gardening hacks will help you grow more food, improve soil health, and maximize space—all without breaking the bank.

Seed Starting & Propagation Hacks

1. **Use Recycled Containers** – Yogurt cups, egg cartons, and milk jugs make excellent free seed-starting trays. Punch holes in the bottom for drainage.
2. **Make Soil Blocks** – Skip the plastic trays by making seed-starting soil blocks using a homemade press. This prevents transplant shock and eliminates waste.
3. **Winter Sow in Milk Jugs** – Cut milk jugs in half, fill them with soil, and plant seeds inside. The jugs act as mini-greenhouses, making them perfect for cold-season starts.
4. **Pre-Sprout Seeds on Paper Towels** – Place seeds between damp paper towels to speed up germination before planting.
5. **Root Cuttings in Water** – Instead of buying new plants, propagate herbs, tomatoes, and berries by placing cuttings in water until roots form.
6. **Save and Swap Seeds** – Harvest seeds from your best plants each year or participate in seed swaps to get free varieties.
7. **Use Cinnamon to Prevent Damping Off** – Sprinkling cinnamon on seedlings helps prevent fungal diseases.
8. **Grow Potatoes in Containers** – Use buckets, bags, or even old tires to grow potatoes vertically and save space.

Soil & Fertilizer Hacks

9. **Make Compost for Free** – Collect kitchen scraps, grass clippings, and leaves to create nutrient-rich compost instead of buying fertilizers.
10. **Use Coffee Grounds** – Add used coffee grounds to the soil for a slow-release nitrogen boost.
11. **Brew Compost Tea** – Soak compost in water for 24 hours and use the nutrient-rich liquid to feed plants.
12. **Make Banana Peel Fertilizer** – Soak banana peels in water for a potassium-rich fertilizer.
13. **Crush Eggshells for Calcium** – Dry and crush eggshells to add calcium to the soil, preventing blossom-end rot in tomatoes and peppers.
14. **Use Epsom Salt for Magnesium** – Dissolve a tablespoon of Epsom salt in a gallon of water and spray on plants to promote growth.
15. **Plant Nitrogen-Fixing Cover Crops** – Clover and peas add nitrogen to the soil naturally, reducing the need for commercial fertilizers.
16. **Mulch with Grass Clippings** – Retain moisture and suppress weeds by using fresh grass clippings as mulch.
17. **Dig Trench Composting** – Bury kitchen scraps directly in garden beds to improve soil without needing a compost pile.
18. **Make Wood Ash Fertilizer** – Sprinkle fireplace ash around plants to add potassium and calcium.

Water Conservation Hacks

19. **Use Olla Pots for Deep Watering** – Bury unglazed clay pots near plants and fill them with water for slow, consistent moisture.

20. **Mulch Heavily** – A thick layer of mulch reduces evaporation and keeps soil moist longer.
21. **Save Rainwater** – Collect rainwater in barrels to water your garden for free.
22. **Reuse Kitchen Water** – Water plants with leftover cooking or dishwater (without soap).
23. **Plant in Trenches** – Dig shallow trenches to direct water to plant roots instead of letting it run off.
24. **Group Plants by Water Needs** – Place thirsty plants together and drought-tolerant plants separately to optimize watering.

Weed & Pest Control Hacks

25. **Suppress Weeds with Cardboard** – Lay cardboard over weedy areas, then cover with mulch to smother unwanted growth.
26. **Use Vinegar as a Natural Weed Killer** – Spray vinegar on weeds in walkways and driveways (avoid using it near plants).
27. **Plant Trap Crops** – Grow sacrificial plants like nasturtiums to attract pests away from vegetables.
28. **Spray DIY Insecticidal Soap** – Mix dish soap with water and spray on plants to control aphids and mites.
29. **Grow Marigolds for Pest Control** – Their scent repels nematodes, whiteflies, and other pests.
30. **Use Diatomaceous Earth** – Sprinkle around plants to deter slugs and insects naturally.
31. **Encourage Beneficial Insects** – Attract ladybugs and lacewings by planting dill, fennel, and alyssum.
32. **Make Beer Traps for Slugs** – Bury shallow containers filled with beer to attract and drown slugs.

DIY Garden Structures & Tools

33. **Build Raised Beds from Pallets** – Disassemble wooden pallets and repurpose them into raised garden beds.
34. **Make a Greenhouse from Salvaged Windows** – Old windows can be turned into a low-cost cold frame or mini-greenhouse.
35. **Use Bamboo or Branches for Trellises** – Instead of buying trellises, tie together branches or bamboo for climbing plants.
36. **Repurpose Old Fencing for Plant Supports** – Wire fencing makes an excellent cucumber or tomato trellis.
37. **DIY Row Covers from Old Sheets** – Protect plants from frost by covering them with repurposed bedsheets.
38. **Create a Drip Irrigation System from Bottles** – Poke holes in a plastic bottle, bury it near plants, and fill it with water for slow-release watering.
39. **Use PVC Pipes for Hoop Houses** – Bend PVC pipes over garden beds and cover them with plastic for a budget-friendly season extender.

Harvesting & Food Preservation Hacks

40. **Store Root Vegetables in Sand** – Keep carrots, potatoes, and beets fresh longer by storing them in damp sand.
41. **Freeze Herbs in Ice Cube Trays** – Chop fresh herbs, place them in ice cube trays with water, and freeze for easy use later.
42. **Make a DIY Solar Dehydrator** – Use a simple wood-and-mesh setup to dry fruits and vegetables without electricity.
43. **Hang Drying Racks for Herbs** – Tie herb bundles and hang them upside down in a dry place to preserve flavor.
44. **Ferment Vegetables for Long-Term Storage** – Make sauerkraut, kimchi, or pickles without expensive canning equipment.

Creative & Upcycling Hacks

45. **Use Old Boots as Planters** – Turn worn-out boots into quirky, rustic garden containers.
46. **Repurpose Broken Pots for Drainage** – Crushed ceramic pots can be used as drainage material at the bottom of containers.
47. **Turn Plastic Bottles into Mini Greenhouses** – Cut the tops off large plastic bottles and place them over seedlings for warmth and protection.
48. **Use Wine Corks for Plant Markers** – Write plant names on corks and place them on skewers for durable, waterproof markers.
49. **Make a Vertical Garden from a Shoe Organizer** – Hang a fabric shoe organizer and plant herbs in each pocket for a space-saving garden.
50. **Convert Old Drawers into Raised Beds** – Fill discarded wooden drawers with soil for instant raised garden beds.
51. **Use an Old Ladder as a Tiered Planter** – Lean a wooden ladder against a wall and place potted plants on each step to maximize growing space.

THE BEST FREE & CHEAP GARDENING RESOURCES (Websites, Books, Groups)

Gardening knowledge has never been more accessible. Whether you're looking for expert advice, free seeds, or a supportive community, there are countless resources available—many of them at little to no cost. Below are some of the best free and budget-friendly gardening resources to help you grow more while spending less.

Free & Budget-Friendly Gardening Websites

1. Cooperative Extension Websites

Every U.S. state has a Cooperative Extension program that provides free research-based gardening advice. These sites offer region-specific growing guides, pest control tips, and soil management techniques.

- Find your local Extension office at nifa.usda.gov/extension.

2. Permies.com

A goldmine of DIY and permaculture gardening discussions. Learn about no-dig gardening, soil health, and food forests from experienced growers worldwide.

3. Dave's Garden (davesgarden.com)

This website features plant databases, forums, and the "Garden Watchdog" section, where gardeners review online seed companies.

4. The Old Farmer's Almanac (almanac.com/gardening)

Offers a free online planting calendar, frost date calculator, and a range of gardening tips.

5. GardenWeb Forums (houzz.com/gardenweb)

One of the largest gardening communities online, covering everything from vegetable gardening to organic pest control.

6. Plants for a Future (pfaf.org)

A free database of over 7,000 useful plants, many of which are edible, medicinal, or great for permaculture gardens.

7. Seed Savers Exchange (seedsavers.org)

While Seed Savers sells seeds, they also provide free guides on heirloom seed saving and plant preservation.

Free & Cheap Gardening Books

Many public libraries offer gardening books for free, and some classic titles are even available online for free. Here are a few highly recommended options:

Free Online Gardening Books

- **"Farmers' Bulletin" (USDA Archive)** – Free historical gardening and farming guides from the U.S. Department of Agriculture. Available at naldc.nal.usda.gov.
- **"One-Straw Revolution" by Masanobu Fukuoka** – A foundational book on natural farming and no-till gardening, often available in public domain archives.
- **"Square Foot Gardening" by Mel Bartholomew** – This method teaches you how to grow more in less space, often found in library book sales or as used copies for a few dollars.
- **"Edible Forest Gardens" by Dave Jacke** – A must-read for those interested in permaculture and food forests.

Low-Cost Gardening Books Worth Buying

If you're willing to invest a little, these books offer great value for the money:

- **"The Resilient Gardener" by Carol Deppe** – Focuses on growing staple crops in a low-cost, self-sufficient way.
- **"Gaia's Garden" by Toby Hemenway** – An affordable introduction to permaculture principles.

- **"How to Grow More Vegetables" by John Jeavons** – One of the best books on biointensive gardening, helping you produce maximum yields in small spaces.

Best Free & Low-Cost Gardening Groups

1. Facebook Gardening Groups

Facebook has numerous gardening communities where members share tips, swap seeds, and offer free resources. Some popular groups include:

- **Backyard Permaculture** – Focuses on sustainable, low-cost gardening methods.
- **Vegetable Garden Hints & Tips** – A friendly community for new and experienced gardeners.
- **Seed Swap USA (or local versions)** – Great for trading seeds and cuttings for free.

2. Reddit Gardening Communities

Reddit hosts active gardening discussions where you can ask questions and get free advice. Some useful subreddits include:

- **r/gardening** – General gardening discussions.
- **r/permaculture** – Focused on sustainable and regenerative gardening.
- **r/seedswap** – A place to trade seeds with gardeners worldwide.

3. Local Gardening Clubs & Seed Libraries

Check your local library, community center, or botanical garden for gardening clubs and seed libraries. Many provide free workshops, plant swaps, and access to free seeds.

4. Freecycle & Buy Nothing Groups

Websites like Freecycle.org and Buy Nothing Facebook groups allow you to find free gardening tools, seeds, and plants from people in your area.

5. Master Gardener Programs

Many universities offer free gardening classes through their Master Gardener programs. These often include free lectures, plant clinics, and even volunteer opportunities where you can learn hands-on.

52-weeks Garden Expense Tracker & Budgeting Worksheets

This structured tracker helps you manage gardening expenses, set a budget, and identify savings opportunities.

GARDEN BUDGETING WORKSHEET

Category	Estimated Budget ($)	Actual Spent ($)	Notes
Seeds & Plants	_____	_____	_____
Soil & Amendments	_____	_____	_____

Tools & Equipment	_____	_____	_____
Water & Utilities	_____	_____	_____
Miscellaneous	_____	_____	_____
Total Budget	_____	_____	_____

Savings Goals & Cost-Saving Strategies

Savings Goal	Target Amount ($)	Strategies to Achieve It
_____	_____	DIY projects, plant propagation, free resources, etc.

30-Day Garden Expense Tracker

Date	Expense Description	Cost ($)	Category	Notes (DIY, Free Finds, Discounts, etc.)
Week 1	_____	_____	_____	_____
Week 2	_____	_____	_____	_____
Week 3	_____	_____	_____	_____
Week 4	_____	_____	_____	_____
Week 5	_____	_____	_____	_____
Week 6	_____	_____	_____	_____
Week 7	_____	_____	_____	_____
Week 8	_____	_____	_____	_____
Week 9	_____	_____	_____	_____

Week 10 _____ _____ _____ _____

Week 11 _____ _____ _____ _____

Week 12 _____ _____ _____ _____

Week 13 _____ _____ _____ _____

Week 14 _____ _____ _____ _____

Week 15 _____ _____ _____ _____

Week 16 _____ _____ _____ _____

Week 17 _____ _____ _____ _____

Week 18 _____ _____ _____ _____

Week 19 _____ _____ _____ _____

Week 20 _____ _____ _____ _____

Week 21 _____ _____ _____ _____

Week 22 _____ _____ _____ _____

Week 23 _____ _____ _____ _____

Week 24 _____ _____ _____ _____

Week 25 _____ _____ _____ _____

Week 26 _____ _____ _____ _____

Week 27 _____ _____ _____ _____

Week 28 _____ _____ _____ _____

Week 29 _____ _____ _____ _____

Week 30 _____ _____ _____ _____

Week 31 _____ _____ _____ _____

Week 32   _____   _____   _____   _____

Week 33   _____   _____   _____   _____

Week 34   _____   _____   _____   _____

Week 35   _____   _____   _____   _____

Week 36   _____   _____   _____   _____

Week 37   _____   _____   _____   _____

Week 38   _____   _____   _____   _____

Week 39   _____   _____   _____   _____

Week 40   _____   _____   _____   _____

Wcek 41   _____   _____   _____   _____

Week 42   _____   _____   _____   _____

Week 43   _____   _____   _____   _____

Week 44   _____   _____   _____   _____

Week 45   _____   _____   _____   _____

Week 46   _____   _____   _____   _____

Week 47   _____   _____   _____   _____

Week 48   _____   _____   _____   _____

Week 49   _____   _____   _____   _____

Week 50   _____   _____   _____   _____

Week 51   _____   _____   _____   _____

Week 52   _____   _____   _____   _____

End-of-Month Summary & Adjustments

Category	Planned Budget ($)	Actual Spent ($)	Over/Under ($)	Adjustments for Next Month
Seeds & Plants	_____	_____	_____	_____
Soil & Amendments	_____	_____	_____	_____
Tools & Equipment	_____	_____	_____	_____
Water & Utilities	_____	_____	_____	_____
Miscellaneous	_____	_____	_____	_____
Total	_____	_____	_____	_____

Reflection: Cost-Saving Wins & Improvements

Category	Successes (Free, DIY, Discounts Used)	Lessons & Adjustments
Seeds	_____	_____
Soil	_____	_____
Tools	_____	_____
Water	_____	_____

This tracker provides a clear, organized way to manage gardening expenses while identifying budget-friendly opportunities.

A YEAR OF GARDEN PROJECTS USING SALVAGED & FREE MATERIALS

This structured guide provides month-by-month DIY garden projects using salvaged, upcycled, and free materials, helping you build a sustainable and cost-effective garden year-round.

January: Planning & Gathering Materials

Project	Materials Needed (Free/Salvaged Sources)	Notes
Design a Garden Layout	Recycled paper, cardboard for sketches	Use online free garden planners
Build a Seed Starting Setup	Upcycled containers (yogurt cups, egg cartons), plastic lids	Start collecting ahead of spring
Insulate Raised Beds for Cold Weather	Bubble wrap, old blankets, straw	Protect overwintering crops

February: DIY Seed Starting & Greenhouse Ideas

Project	Materials Needed (Free/Salvaged Sources)	Notes
Make a Mini Greenhouse	Salvaged windows, clear plastic bins	Repurpose old storm windows
DIY Heat Mat Alternative	String lights, bricks, cardboard	Helps with germination indoors
Create Seed Starting Pots	Newspaper, toilet paper rolls, eggshells	Biodegradable and zero-cost

March: Soil Building & Garden Structure Setup

Project	Materials Needed (Free/Salvaged Sources)	Notes
Build a No-Cost Compost Bin	Pallets, chicken wire, trash cans	Start decomposing

		organic waste early
Make Leaf Mold for Soil Health	Fall leaves, wire mesh	Nature's free soil amendment
Construct Raised Beds	Salvaged wood, bricks, logs	Look for discarded wood locally

April: Smart Planting & Water Conservation

Project	Materials Needed (Free/Salvaged Sources)	Notes
DIY Drip Irrigation	Old hoses, plastic bottles	Reduce water waste
Create a Rainwater Collection System	Food-grade barrels, downspouts	Cut water costs significantly

Project	Materials Needed	Notes
Repurpose Old Fencing for Trellises	Wire mesh, wooden pallets	Support climbing plants

May: DIY Trellises & Pest Control

Project	Materials Needed (Free/Salvaged Sources)	Notes
Build Upcycled Trellises	Old bed frames, bike rims, wooden stakes	Supports cucumbers, peas, and beans
Make Natural Pest Sprays	Garlic, onion, cayenne pepper	Avoid chemical pesticides
Attract Beneficial Insects	Old logs, broken pots, straw bundles	Create habitats for pollinators

June: Vertical Gardening & Summer Protection

Project	Materials Needed (Free/Salvaged Sources)	Notes
Construct Vertical Planters	Pallets, hanging shoe organizers	Maximizes space for small gardens
DIY Shade Covers for Plants	Old sheets, bamboo poles	Protects crops from extreme sun
Mulch for Free	Grass clippings, shredded paper, wood chips	Retains moisture and suppresses weeds

July: Water-Saving & Mid-Season Fixes

Project	Materials Needed (Free/Salvaged Sources)	Notes
Make DIY Olla Pots	Old terracotta pots	Slow-release watering system

Project	Materials Needed	Notes
Build a Greywater Recycling System	Buckets, PVC pipes	Redirect sink/shower water for irrigation
Reinforce Plant Supports	Twine, branches, repurposed netting	Prevents breakage in strong winds

August: Seed Saving & Propagation

Project	Materials Needed (Free/Salvaged Sources)	Notes
DIY Seed Envelopes	Junk mail, paper bags	Store seeds for next season
Propagate Herbs from Cuttings	Water glasses, small containers	Basil, mint, and rosemary root easily
Divide & Replant Perennials	Hand trowel, compost	Free plants for next year

September: Fall Garden Prep & Cold Protection

Project	Materials Needed (Free/Salvaged Sources)	Notes
DIY Row Covers	Plastic bottles, old bed sheets	Protects against early frost
Mulch Paths & Beds	Leaves, straw, wood chips	Suppresses weeds and improves soil
Build Cold Frames	Salvaged windows, bricks, wood	Extend the growing season

October: Winterizing & Garden Cleanup

Project	Materials Needed (Free/Salvaged Sources)	Notes

Project	Materials Needed	Notes
Insulate Raised Beds	Bubble wrap, burlap sacks	Keep soil warm for winter crops
Make a No-Turn Compost Pile	Pile of leaves, grass clippings	Decomposes slowly over winter
Upcycle Old Containers for Storage	Buckets, milk crates	Store bulbs, tools, and seeds

November: Indoor Gardening & Tool Maintenance

Project	Materials Needed (Free/Salvaged Sources)	Notes
Regrow Vegetables Indoors	Kitchen scraps, water glasses	Lettuce, green onions, and celery regrow easily
Clean & Oil Garden Tools	Sand, motor oil, old rags	Extends tool life for next season

| Make DIY Plant Labels | Popsicle sticks, broken blinds | Keep track of overwintering crops |

December: Reflection & Planning Ahead

Project	Materials Needed (Free/Salvaged Sources)	Notes
Review Garden Successes	Notebook, saved receipts	Adjust budget and plans for next year
Start a Winter Indoor Garden	Plastic containers, soil mix	Grow microgreens and herbs
Find Free & Discounted Seeds	Online seed swaps, community groups	Plan ahead for the next growing season

This structured, month-by-month guide ensures you maximize free and salvaged materials throughout the year, making gardening both affordable and sustainable.

www.ingramcontent.com/pod-product-compliance
Ingram Content Group UK Ltd.
Pitfield, Milton Keynes, MK11 3LW, UK
UKHW020648300825
7649UKWH00003B/377